AMAZING CAT STORIES

101 Unforgettable Cats Who Shaped History and Left Their Paw Prints on the World

KAREN ROBERTS

ISBN: 978-1-957590-45-5

For questions, email: Support@AwesomeReads.org

Please consider writing a review!

Just visit: AwesomeReads.org/review

Copyright 2024. All Rights Reserved.

No part of this book may be reproduced or transmitted in any form or by any means, electronic or mechanical, including photocopying, recording, or by any other form without written permission from the publisher.

FREE BONUS

SCAN TO GET OUR NEXT BOOK FOR FREE!

Table of Contents

INTRODUCTION 1
CHAPTER ONE: INTERNET CATS 3
   [1] ABLE THE "TWO-LEGGED CAT" 4
   [2] COLONEL MEOW 5
   [3] HAMILTON THE HIPSTER CAT 6
   [4] KEYBOARD CAT 7
   [5] LIL BUB 8
   [6] MARU 9
   [7] NALA CAT 10
   [8] NYAN CAT 11
   [9] PUSHEEN 12
   [10] SMUDGE THE CAT 13
   [11] SOCKINGTON 14
   [12] TARA 15
   [13] TARDAR SAUCE AKA "GRUMPY CAT" 16

CHAPTER TWO: CATS IN POLITICS 19
   [14] INDIA "WILLIE" 20
   [15] LARRY 21
   [16] MISTY MALARKY YING YANG 22
   [17] PALMERSTON 24
   [18] SOCKS 25
   [19] STUBBS 26

CHAPTER THREE: ADVENTUROUS CATS 29
   [20] EMILY 30
   [21] FÉLICETTE 31
   [22] MRS. CHIPPY 32

[23] TRIM 34
[24] WILLOW 35

CHAPTER FOUR: WORKING CATS 37

[25] BLACKIE 38
[26] D-O-G (DEE-OH-JEE) 39
[27] FRED THE UNDERCOVER KITTY 40
[28] OSCAR 41
[29] SNOWBALL 42
[30] TAMA 44
[31] UNSINKABLE SAM 45

CHAPTER FIVE: ACTING CATS 47

[32] DEMETER 48
[33] GOOSE 48
[34] JONESY 49
[35] MORRIS 51
[36] MR. BIGGLESWORTH 52
[37] MR. JINX 53
[38] SASSY 54
[39] THACKERAY BINX 55
[40] TONTO 56

CHAPTER SIX: CARTOON CATS 59

[41] BERLIOZ, TOULOUSE, AND MARIE 60
[42] CATBUS 61
[43] DUCHESS 62
[44] FIGARO 64
[45] JIJI 65
[46] LUCIFER 66
[47] MR. WHISKERS 67
[48] MUFASA 68

[49] OLIVER 69
[50] SI AND AM 70
[51] SIMBA 71
[52] THOMAS O'MALLEY 72

CHAPTER SEVEN: CATS ON THE TELLY 75

[53] ARTEMIS 76
[54] BABBIT AND CATSTELLO 77
[55] CATDOG 78
[56] DIANA 79
[57] FELIX THE CAT 79
[58] HELLO KITTY 80
[59] JIBANYAN 82
[60] LUNA 83
[61] MEOWTH 84
[62] SALEM SABERHAGEN 85
[63] SCRATCHY 86
[64] SMELLY CAT 87
[65] SNARF 87
[66] SNOWBALL I, II, III, IV, AND V 89
[67] SPOT 90
[68] SYLVESTER 91
[69] TOM 92
[70] TOP CAT 94

CHAPTER EIGHT: COMIC CATS 97

[71] AZRAEL 98
[72] GARFIELD 99
[73] HEATHCLIFF 100
[74] HOBBES 102
[75] KRAZY KAT 103
[76] LYING CAT 104

CHAPTER NINE: LITERARY CATS 107

[77] BAGHEERA 108
[78] BOB THE STREET CAT 109
[79] CROOKSHANKS 110
[80] HODGE 111
[81] MACAVITY 112
[82] MATILDA 113
[83] MRS. NORRIS 114
[84] PUSS IN BOOTS 115
[85] SNOWBELL 117
[86] THE CAT IN THE HAT 118
[87] THE CHESHIRE CAT 119
[88] TIGGER 121

CHAPTER TEN: OTHER NEWSWORTHY CATS 123

[89] ALL BALL 124
[90] BART, THE ZOMBIE CAT 125
[91] BLACKIE THE TALKING CAT 126
[92] CASPER 127
[93] CC (CARBON COPY) 129
[94] CHOUPETTE 130
[95] CRÈME PUFF 131
[96] LITTLE NICKY 132
[97] PETER, THE LORD'S CAT 133
[98] POOH 133
[99] RIJKA 135
[100] TOMMASO 135
[101] WADSWORTH 136

CONCLUSION 139

INTRODUCTION

Cats have always been an important part of our lives, capturing our hearts and imaginations for thousands of years. We've had a fascination with our feline companions from the time of the earliest recorded civilizations. Their unbelievable cuteness, mischievousness, and independence make cats an eternal favorite, once worshiped in ancient civilizations and now dominating social media feeds.

The relationship between humans and cats can be traced back to ancient times. In fact, the first evidence of cat and human relationships dates back over 9,500 years when a grave was discovered containing a cat buried with its human. Cats were later revered as sacred animals in ancient Egypt, believed to possess divine powers and often mummified after death to be buried with their human companions. In many cultures, cats were seen as symbols of good luck and protection.

However, it isn't just their cuteness that has made cats a favorite of humans; they also provide a valuable service in keeping rodents at bay. Their usefulness is another reason why cats are heavily featured in art, literature, and mythology.

It's time to meet some of the cats who have achieved incredible feats, cats who have made significant contributions to society, and cats who have simply captured our hearts with their extraordinary personalities. From space to sea, comic strips to the big screen, cats have taken over and left their mark on history and pop culture. Below, we will delve into the most popular furry icons and their unique stories, the reasons behind their enduring popularity, and the continuing fascination that these creatures hold for us. Here are 101 of the most famous cats in the world:

CHAPTER ONE: INTERNET CATS

[1]
ABLE THE "TWO-LEGGED CAT"

Born as a stray in Thailand, Able learned that he had to hunt for his food. One fateful day, a tragic hunting accident occurred while Able was chasing a bird across rooftops; he slipped and fell off the roof. He landed on his feet, but unfortunately, it was on an electrical power line. While bystanders rushed to save him, severe damage had already been done.

To survive, Able's front two legs and part of his rear had to be removed. After he survived the procedure, no one was willing to take Able in. He was returned to the streets to live as an alley cat with only two back legs.

Thankfully, a lady noticed him and was immediately inspired to take him home. Able now lives with another disabled cat that can't use its back legs, but they are best friends. Able's name reflects his extraordinary ability, and his new owner now shares Able's amazing feats on social media, such as him hopping, running on his back legs, and jumping.

Interesting Fact: With no tail or front feet, Able is still capable of going up and down stairs.

[2]
COLONEL MEOW

Another Guinness World Record holder and internet favorite is Colonel Meow. He temporarily held the 2014 world record for the longest hair on a cat, measuring in at a whopping nine inches, and was well known for his looks on the internet.

Born October 11, 2011, Colonel Meow was with the Seattle Himalayan and Persian Society and was adopted by Anne Marie Avey from a local Petco. Anne Marie started posting pictures online and Colonel Meow quickly gained fame for his funny looks and fluffy hair.

Colonel Meow was a social media sensation with millions of followers on various social sites. While the pictures often depicted him as a grumpy-looking fella, he was actually quite friendly and loving. The funny captions that Anne posted on his pictures depicted him as an adorable, yet fearsome, dictator.

Unfortunately, Colonel Meow's celebrity status was cut short when it was discovered he had heart problems requiring surgery and a blood transfusion. He died tragically of cardiac arrest due to infection and kidney failure at only two years old. Although he was a short-lived celebrity, he is still held dear in the hearts of internet users everywhere.

Interesting Fact: Colonel's unique mix of Himalayan and Persian breeds was responsible for his record-setting long hair.

[3]
HAMILTON THE HIPSTER CAT

Another internet sensation known for his distinctive facial features is Hamilton the Hipster Cat. Originally a feral cat, Hamilton was adopted from an animal shelter by Jay Stowe. When Stowe first met Hamilton, he was hiding at the back of the cage and rather skittish.

For the first month of his life with Jay, Hamilton hid in the bathroom and spent another month in the closet. Finally, he felt comfortable enough to cuddle with Jay, which is when his owner noticed Hamilton's unique appearance. He had a white "mustache" that looked exactly like the mustaches so popular among hipsters at the time, so Jay started posting photos. Due to his mustache, fluffy coat, and bright green eyes, Hamilton, affectionately nicknamed "Hammy," received over 100 likes in ten minutes on his first photo.

Hammy was such a playful cat that it was easy for Jay to get a host of wonderful pictures of him, often posing him with hipster paraphernalia. In fact, managing Hamilton's account became a full-time job because he was so popular. Hamilton went on to build a massive following on Instagram, star in a web series, appear in commercials, and even had calendars made from his photos. There was even an app where you could add Hamilton to your pictures, which was useful since Hamilton didn't make any public appearances due to his fear of crowds.

After reaching great success and getting 550,000 followers on Instagram, Hamilton's account was donated to charity to help raise money for high-kill shelters like the one Hammy was rescued from. Now, Hamilton is moving at a slower pace in the later phase of his life. As of 2021, he was still doing well and enjoying life with his loving family.

Interesting Fact: Hammy was found on the streets of San Jose and brought in by a volunteer to the Silicon Valley Humane Society.

[4]
KEYBOARD CAT

Originally filmed in 1984, Fatso the Cat would become internet famous for his seeming ability to play the keyboard.

The video was filmed by Charlie Schmidt and featured Fatso playing an electric keyboard wearing a light blue baby shirt while a cheery tune played in the background. In 2007, Charlie uploaded the video onto YouTube. Although Fatso had passed away in 1987, the VHS tape of her kept her memory alive.

While Fatso wasn't actually playing the keyboard and was instead manipulated by Charlie, the results were so great no one cared. Charlie created the video out of boredom and had no idea how famous it would become twenty years after Fatso had passed away. The digitized version of the video was uploaded in June 2007 under the title "Charlie Schmidt's 'Cool Cat,' but once it began to grow in fame and popularity, he renamed the video "Charlie Schmidt's Keyboard Cat! – THE ORIGINAL!" In October of the same year, the video had over 73 million views.

Since Fatso passed away, Charlie has had other keyboard cats, but none with the fame that Fatso acquired.

Interesting Fact: The song was featured on Brad O'Farrell's website as a blooper to "play" people offstage when they messed up.

[5]
LIL BUB

Lil Bub is another well-known internet-famous kitty. Her unique looks and sweet personality made her an icon for animal welfare everywhere and stole the hearts of her fans.

She was born on June 21, 2011, the runt of an otherwise healthy litter of feral kittens. Lil Bub was found in a tool shed in the middle of rural Indiana during the summer. She was taken in by Mike Bridavsky because of all the special care she would need to keep her alive and healthy. When Mike first met her, he called her "Bub" and the name stuck.

Lil Bub suffered from a form of feline dwarfism that caused her to remain almost kitten-sized her entire life. She also had extra toes on each foot, and a short lower jaw that prevented her from being able to keep her tongue in her mouth. Along with her physical disabilities, she suffered from osteopetrosis for which she had to take medication.

When owner Mike posted pictures and videos of her on social media, she quickly became popular because of her unique appearance. She became well known for her tongue hanging out, large eyes, and adorable personality. Lil Bub quickly attracted millions of adoring fans.

The more famous Lil Bub became, the more she developed into an advocate for animal welfare and a symbol of acceptance. Mike used her stardom to raise awareness for different animal causes including adoption, spaying, neutering, and special needs animals. Lil Bub also worked with different organizations to raise hundreds of thousands of dollars for animals.

During her amazing life, she appeared on *Lil Bub & Friendz*, *Good Morning America*, *The View*, and *The Ellen DeGeneres Show*. All these appearances led to plush toys, clothing, and a wide variety of other merchandise that fans could purchase. A portion of the profit from all the sales went to charities and other organizations.

On December 1, 2019, Lil Bub passed away from an infection in her bones relating to osteoporosis. Her fans were devastated and mourn her still.

Interesting Fact: During her lifetime, Lil Bub raised over $700,000 to help other animals in need of special treatment.

[6]
MARU

Maru is a well-known male Scottish Fold cat from Japan who started gaining popularity after his first video was released in September 2016. Maru's ears are folded forward, making him look owl-like. Like all Scottish Folds, he is extremely affectionate and friendly.

Maru's owner figured out the perfect way to keep him entertained and out of trouble by posting videos under the "mugumogu" account name. Every Friday, they would upload a new video of Maru playing with boxes and showing off his fun personality. Maru was born in May 2007 and by July 2007, his owner knew he was something special, prompting Maru's owner to share him with the world.

Just three years later, Maru became a TV star when he appeared in a Japanese pet food commercial. He was also featured in books and magazines. Because of the exposure, Scottish Folds as a breed have become more popular and much more in demand.

Maru's videos have been viewed over 535 million times, at one point earning him the title of the most YouTube videos as an individual animal in the *Guinness Book of World Records*.

Interesting Fact: Maru means "circle" in Japanese.

[7]
NALA CAT

You've probably seen her picture online. Nala is known for her adorable looks and vivid blue eyes. Born July 28, 2010, she's a Siamese/tabby mix with over 4 million followers on Instagram. She's one of the most famous cats to take the internet by storm.

Nala was in an animal shelter as a kitten where she caught the eye of her owner Varisiri Methachittiphan, or Pooki, to her friends. Pooki adopted Nala and took her home in 2011. An account originally intended for sharing pictures with friends and family started gaining attention when Pooki started posting pictures of Nala.

Nala's followers know her by her funny antics and unique personality. The friendly cat delighted her internet fans with videos of her playing with boxes, sleeping in strange places, and wearing cute outfits. In 2012, Nala's photo was published on *Buzzfeed*, giving the kitty her big break. Nala's cute face, charming personality, and stunning eyes won people over, and her followers continued to grow. It didn't take long before she was appearing on talk shows and in commercials.

Due to her origin story, Nala's owners used her success to raise awareness for shelter animals and adoption. Countless cats have found their forever homes through Nala's online presence and stardom. While conscious of her roots, Nala has come a long way from the shelter-kitten she once was, with a current net worth of $100 million. But Nala doesn't stop there — she is also a certified therapy cat.

Interesting Fact: Nala holds the Guinness World Record for the most followers on Instagram with over 4.3 million followers.

[8]
NYAN CAT

The Nyan Cat became well known for its YouTube video that became internet famous as a meme. The video was released with a Japanese Pop Song that features the pop-tart body of Nyan.

Nyan looks like a pop-tart with a cat tail, cat feet, and a cat head. When Nyan cat flies around, it leaves rainbows in its wake. The iconic cat was created by 25-year-old Christopher Torres, or "prguitarman," his internet handle. Torres created the idea when he was working at a blood drive and someone asked him to draw a cat followed by a pop-tart, leading him to combine the two. Even with the strange inspiration, there was a real-life cat who helped Nyan come to life. This was Marty Torres's cat who passed away in 2012 from feline infectious peritonitis.

The popular song in the background of the video was called "Nyanyanyanyanyanya!" The word nya is a Japanese onomatopoeic. An onomatopoeic sounds just like it is spelled. and in this case, nya is the Japanese version of "meow." The song was uploaded onto a Japanese site called Niconico by user "daniwell."

Interesting Fact: The creator of Nyan Cat, Christopher Torres, and the creator of Keyboard Cat, Charles Schmidt, sued Warner Bros for using their images and characters without compensating them. They settled in 2013 and got paid for their unique characters.

[9]
PUSHEEN

Pusheen is an iconic "tubby tabby" that has become famous for her stickers, comics, and images used on Facebook, messages, and most platforms.

When sending a text, her cute Graphics Interchange Formats (GIFs) and stickers make any message adorable. Pusheen is brought to life by Pusheen Corp., an Illinois company that was founded in 2010. Since opening, Pusheen Corp. has received over 100 licenses globally and expanded into numerous markets.

Pusheen's first appearance was in a 2010 comic that was created by the two founders of Pusheen Corp, Claire Belton and Andrew Duff. They created a Tumblr blog that was immensely popular and shared hundreds of thousands of times. In 2013, the comic *I am Pusheen the Cat* was printed by Simon & Schuster and has expanded into twelve different languages.

While all of this was taking place, Facebook was working on releasing their chat stickers and Pusheen was made into emoji-style stickers that everyone wanted to use. It's thought that over 20 billion Pusheen images have been sent across all social media platforms, ensuring her popularity.

According to her website, she has all nine lives left and her best feature is her bean-like toes. Pusheen is known to be both lazy and curious and is a gray tabby cat that is extremely overweight with a sweet disposition.

Interesting Fact: Pusheen's birthday is February 18th, making her an Aquarius.

[10]
SMUDGE THE CAT

A British shorthair from Ottawa, Ontario, Smudge is known for becoming internet famous as a meme. The solid white cat was captured making a face at a salad in June 2018. The picture was uploaded and became a sensation for his relatable expression.

After a few months of sitting on owner Miranda Stillabower's Tumblr page, the photo was eventually shared tens of thousands of times. Someone then paired Smudge's picture with an angry housewife from *The Real Housewives* franchise, and it grew even more popular.

Smudge's popularity continued to grow with over 1 million followers, but despite his fame, Miranda claims that the cat is still clueless. Smudge is just a cat going about cat business. He does make a regular appearance at the dinner table and expects a chair to be left open for him, which allows Miranda to snap more pictures of the cute kitty.

Miranda would like to take Smudge around to meet his fans, but unfortunately, he suffers from anxiety. Until a behavioral therapist can help Smudge overcome his anxiety, he'll be staying at home.

Interesting Fact: When Smudge got over 1 million followers, it made him one of the most popular celebrities in his area, outpacing the area's most famous dog.

[11]
SOCKINGTON

Becoming famous on Twitter, Sockington came into the public eye in 2007 when his owner Jason Scott started posting cute pictures of him online.

Starting life out as a stray frequenting near a subway station in Boston, Sockington was saved in 2004. He was all gray with a white tuxedo print and white socks. His socks also earned him the nickname Sockamillion. By 2018, Sockington had over 1.2 million followers, many of them animals like him.

All of his tweets were presented from his perspective, and he was described by Mary Ullmer of *The Grand Rapids Press* as "Garfield goes 21st century." He remained popular and passed away in July of 2022.

Interesting Fact: Jason Scott also had two other cats that he put on Twitter, Pennycat and Tweetie.

[12]
TARA

A brave tabby named Tara became a hero in May 2014 by protecting part of her adopted family from a vicious dog attack. In 2008, the Triantafilo family welcomed Tara into their home after she followed them home and quickly became part of the family. Six years later, autistic four-year-old Jeremy was playing with his bike in the driveway when a neighbor's dog attacked.

The dog was an eight-month-old Lab Chow mix that grabbed Jeremy's leg and started pulling the little boy down the driveway. Tara came charging out of nowhere and attacked the dog, scaring it off before returning to check on Jeremy.

It just so happened that a security camera caught the entire incident. The family uploaded the video to YouTube where it received over 16.8 million views in just two days. Tara went on to win the Cat Fanciers' Association's Cat Hero Award, the Special Award for Cat Achievement from Cat Vid Festival, the military dog Blue Tiger Award, and the Los Angeles SPCA's Hero Dog award. Tara also became the grand marshal of a local Christmas parade, and an entire day was dedicated in her honor.

Interesting Fact: Tara's full name is Zatara inspired by The Count of Monte Cristo.

[13]
TARDAR SAUCE
AKA "GRUMPY CAT"

The iconic cat is adored by internet users for her unique look. She was born on April 4, 2012, and became known by her fans as Grumpy Cat. The internet celebrity suffered from feline dwarfism (only seen in 1 out of every 15,000 cats) and an underbite, which led to her having a permanently grumpy expression on her face.

Grumpy Cat's real name was Tardar Sauce, because owner Tabatha Bundesen thought her dark, speckled fur as a kitten bore a striking resemblance to tartar sauce. The misspelled comparison stuck, and so Grumpy Cat was called Tard for short.

Tabatha clearly loved her cat, which was one of four kittens born to a calico short-haired mother and a gray and white striped father. While smaller than her siblings, Grumpy Cat would go on to do great things.

Her first debut on the internet was when a picture was posted by Tabatha's brother to Reddit where it quickly became a favorite. The picture was of Grumpy Cat at five months old and was quickly upvoted by tens of thousands of people in just 24 hours.

When speculation started bubbling up that Grumpy Cat was nothing more than a photoshopped cutie, Tabatha posted videos of the unique cat, who got more than 1.5 million views in the first 36 hours alone.

Grumpy Cat's Facebook page had 7 million followers by the end of 2014, her YouTube videos had collected 2.4 million followers, and she had a significant presence on Twitter and Instagram as well.

Grumpy Cat went on to be on the cover of *The Wall Street Journal* in May of 2013, the cover of *New York Magazine* in October of 2013, and was the feature of several books. Her books included *Grumpy Cat: A Grumpy Book* (which was on *The New York Times* Best Seller list), *The Grumpy Guide to Life: Observations by Grumpy Cat*, and *Grumpy Cat No-It-All: Everything You Need to No*.

She also became the "spokescat" for Friskies and was also featured in a lifetime movie. Her stardom didn't stop there—she went on the talk show circuit making appearances on *Today, Good Morning America,* and *American Idol*. Her face was everywhere, including on t-shirts, cups, and stickers.

Unfortunately, Grumpy Cat's fame was cut short when she passed away on May 17, 2019, at just seven years old due to complications from a UTI. Throughout her seven years, Grumpy Cat was thought to have amassed $99 million.

Interesting Fact: Grumpy Cat won a lawsuit against Grenade Beverage, the makers of Grumppuccino, because they tried to make more drinks than their agreement allowed. She won in California federal court and was awarded $710,000 in damages.

CHAPTER TWO: CATS IN POLITICS

[14]
INDIA "WILLIE"

A solid black American domestic, India lived with the Bush family in the White House while they were there. Originally India went to live with the Bush family when the twin daughters Barbara and Jenna were nine years old.

When the family moved from the governor's mansion to the White House in 2001, India moved with them. While India lived at the White House, she didn't get much attention because the media focused on the family's two Scottish Terriers; Barney and Miss Beazley.

However, that's not to say India went completely without media coverage—she was known for making appearances on the "Barneycams" that were set up to watch the dogs. In 2008, a portrait of India sitting in the White House appeared in *Architectural Digest*.

India passed away at 18 years old, to the sadness of the entire family. India wasn't the star of the media, but she did cause some international issues in the country of India, where they claimed it was disrespectful to name a cat after the country. In fact, the people of Thiruvananthapuram went as far as to burn an effigy of the president to show their disgust. The Bush family did not change their cat's name.

Interesting Fact: India was named after the baseball player Ruben Sierra, who earned the nickname "El Indio" while he played for the Texas Rangers during the time that George Bush owned the team.

[15]
LARRY

Another gainfully employed cat is Larry, a brown and white shorthair tabby who works at the Cabinet Office in London where he is looked after by a doting staff.

Born in 2007, Larry did not start out living the high life, but instead lived out his early years as a stray. He was later picked up by the Battersea Dogs and Cats Home, where he was adopted with the original intent of giving him to former Prime Minister David Cameron's children. However, he was such a good cat, that he earned himself a full-time position.

Since he moved into the Cabinet Office on February 15, 2011, Larry has spent his days "greeting guests to the house, inspecting security defenses, and testing antique furniture for napping quality," according to the home's website.

When Larry first arrived, he caught a mouse on April 22, 2011, and went on to execute another one in August 2012, which he proudly dropped on the front lawn. After he decided he had done enough, he chose to relax until October 2013 when he caught 4 mice in just 2 weeks.

Larry faced fierce competition when Palmerston the cat moved into the Foreign Office next door. Vicious rumors have circulated that Larry spends more time napping than mouse-hunting and might be lacking the killer instinct needed to be a truly great mouse catcher.

In fact, Larry slacked on the job so much he got the nickname Lazy Larry and was temporarily replaced as chief mouser to the Cabinet Office by Freya, who had to be hired in 2012 to control the growing rat population. This enraged Larry so much that a fight had to be broken up between the two by the police. Unfortunately, Freya was not happy with the quiet life at Downing Street and strayed away, only to be hit by a car after two years.

Larry was such a favorite of the public that his every move was closely followed, and he was reported in the press quite often. He was so popular that there was a 15% increase in adoptions at the animal rescue he came from. Ever since Larry arrived, the press would camp outside to try and get footage of him. The public sends Larry treats and gifts often to make sure he knows his efforts are appreciated. Larry is still going strong at 16-years-old, living the good life at Downing Street.

Interesting Fact: Larry was caught on CCTV chasing a fox away in October of 2023, still protecting the area.

[16]
MISTY MALARKY YING YANG

Misty Malarky Ying Yang was a precious Siamese cat who was a member of President Carter's family. Misty the male cat belonged to Amy, the sole daughter of President Jimmy Carter and his wife,

First Lady Rosalynn Carter. Misty was the last cat to live in the White House until Socks moved in.

Misty seemed to be a normal Siamese, often characterized as extremely intelligent, delightfully playful, and always active. Siamese are also known to be very opinionated and talkative. Misty proved this to be true during Amy's piano lessons when he would plant himself in the room to "sing" along, meowing loudly. It's also known that Siamese cats tend to bond strongly with one person and love that person above anyone else. This seemed to be true about Misty and Amy.

While there are many pictures of Misty by himself and with Amy, he wasn't always a fan of photography. The large occasions, like the first state dinner, had Misty wandering down the stairs only to turn back around and go hide when all the cameras started flashing.

Misty was not given free rein of the White House but didn't seem to suffer since he got steak and seafood regularly. One of the most famous pictures of Amy and Misty comes from 1977, where Amy is wearing a flowered dress and holding Misty, who lounges in her arms.

Another famous picture of the two appeared after Amy was arrested for disorderly conduct. She was demonstrating in front of the South African Embassy and got within 500 feet of the building. There were over 1,500 people that were arrested for demonstrating against South Africa's apartheid policy. While her family was proud of her, Amy nevertheless took the time to explain to the press what had happened. During that interview, Misty was in her lap providing moral support.

Interesting Fact: Misty's name was so interesting that Gabor Szabo turned it into a song "Misty Malarky Ying Yang."

[17]
PALMERSTON

A fierce competitor of Larry, Palmerston became the Chief Mouser at the Foreign & Commonwealth Office at Whitehall. A black and white tuxedo cat, Palmerston started his career on April 13, 2016, coming from the same rescue shelter as Larry, Battersea Dogs & Cats Home. He was named after the past Prime Minister Lord Palmerston and was born sometime in 2014.

Palmerston's first big news story came when he caught a mouse on May 3, 2016, and then again when he and Larry got into a standoff on July 11, 2016. In an ever-escalating relationship between Palmerston and Larry, Palmerston was caught sneaking into 10 Downing looking for Larry but was removed by the police before a fight could break out. On August 1, 2016, the inevitable happened and the two got into a serious catfight that caused Palmerston injury to his ear and cost Larry his collar.

By August 2020, Palmerston had put in the time and retired to the countryside to get away from his adoring fans and enjoy his life.

Interesting Fact: Palmerston's Twitter tag is @DiploMog.

[18]
SOCKS

Socks, a tuxedo cat that got his name from his white feet, belonged to former President Clinton and his family. He became famous for being the Clintons' only cat during the early years of Bill Clinton's presidency.

Socks was born around 1989 but didn't join the Clinton family until 1991 when he jumped into the arms of Chelsea Clinton leaving her piano teacher's house. Socks was adopted by the Clintons and his brother Midnight, with whom he was playing the day Chelsea met him, went to another family.

Socks moved into the White House with the family from the governor's mansion and became the first cat and only pet of the Clintons. He played an important role in the family, visiting hospitals and schools, and even led the children's guided tour on the website.

When the Clintons got ready to leave the White House, they unfortunately couldn't take the cat with them because they had adopted a dog, Buddy, and the two did not get along. Thankfully, Betty Currie, Bill Clinton's secretary, chose to take the cat home to Hollywood, Maryland. With Betty and her husband, Socks lived a happy life until 2008 when he developed thyroid problems and died in 2009.

Interesting Fact: Socks was so well known that his obituary was posted in *Time* magazine. He was also the subject of several books written about him including *Dear Socks, Dear Buddy: Kids' Letters to* the First Pets, and Socks Goes to Washington: The Diary of America's First Cat.

[19]
STUBBS

Talkeetna Alaska is a small town known for its wild landscape, dog sledding, and sightseeing, but it's also known for one other unusual fact: the mayor of Talkeetna was a cat.

Stubbs was voted in by write-in election in 1997, when the town of 900 unanimously decided he was the cat for the job! In reality, the town didn't have a mayor, but Stubbs was the closest thing to it as holder of this honorary title. The town decided Stubbs should have the job so that more tourists would come to see the town with a cat in charge. He was flooded with letters and mail, and as many as 30-40 people a day came to the town to meet Stubbs.

Stubbs could be seen every afternoon at a local restaurant drinking his catnip water out of fancy glasses, which was quite a leap from his humble beginning as part of an abandoned litter found in a parking lot. Stubbs' owner, Lauri Stec, quickly picked Stubbs out of all the kittens because he did not have a tail, which is how he ended up getting his name.

Stubbs ruled his domain and did a good enough job that in 2014 there were talks of writing his name in on the senate election. In fact, he had a video criticizing both the Democratic and Republican candidates.

Unfortunately, Mayor Stubbs did not have the perfect life. In 2013, Stubbs was attacked by a dog and rushed to a hospital 70 miles away with a fractured sternum, punctured lung, and a deep laceration on his side. People quickly rallied behind their favorite mayor and money was raised to pay the high vet bills, with the surplus given to an animal shelter. He was also the victim of several other incidents, such as being shot by teenagers with BB guns, falling into a thankfully inoperative deep fryer, and being toted off by a garbage truck.

By 2015, Stubbs the mayor had slowed down and was getting ready to enjoy his later years. He passed away on July 21, 2017, after a fulfilling life at the old age of 20 years and 3 months.

Interesting Fact: Mayor Stubbs' successor is also a cat! This next ruling feline is named Denali, and she took the mantle from Mayor Stubbs after he passed away. A dog was running against Denali at one point, but he disappeared under mysterious circumstances.

CHAPTER THREE: ADVENTUROUS CATS

[20]
EMILY

In 2005, a cat named Emily decided she wanted to try out traveling and snuck into a shipping container that would turn out to go much farther than she planned.

Originally from Wisconsin, Emily disappeared in September and couldn't be found by her nine-year-old owner, Nick Herndon, or any of the other family members. She had wandered into a storage container at a local paper company's warehouse and distribution center. There she snuck into a container full of shipping bales and got locked in.

With Emily inside, the container was sent on a truck to Illinois and then loaded onto a ship. The ship sailed to Belgium where it was opened up and the cat was discovered on Oct 24th in Raflatac, a company in Nancy, France. While Emily was skinny and dehydrated, she was alive.

Thankfully, Emily was wearing a tag with her vet's information on it, so the workers were able to get her back to her family. Emily was sent home first class and handed directly to Nick Herndon. She was flown home compliments of Continental Airlines after a one-month quarantine wait.

While flying home, Emily had no interest in the peppered salmon that was prepared for her and stuck with her French cat food. According to her family, this must have done her a lot of good because she was heavier than ever.

Interesting Fact: Continental Airlines received the title of most pet-friendly airline in 2009.

[21]
FÉLICETTE

While Trim had great navel adventures, another cat by the name of Félicette had an interesting adventure of a different sort; she was the only cat to ever survive in space.

Félicette was found as a stray on the streets of Paris by the Centre d'Enseignement et de Recherches de Médecine Aéronautique (CERMA). Along with Félicette, they collected 13 other cats—all female because they thought the female sex would handle the experience better.

Of all the cats that were picked up, Félicette was the one who stayed the calmest and maintained her weight. In fact, the other cats in the program put on weight while Félicette remained petite. All the cats underwent extensive training just like any astronaut would before being sent into space, including a centrifuge under a high-G scenario with simulated rocket noise to test how they would react.

Félicette was a black and white tuxedo cat who, on October 18, 1963, was eventually sent off into space. She was the first cat to ever enter space and survive as part of a 15-minute suborbital trip that was launched from a base in the Sahara Desert and went all the way up 100 miles above Earth.

The entire time she was out of orbit, scientists monitored her vitals with electrodes that had been planted throughout her body. When it was time, the capsule detached and plummeted back to the ground with a parachute to stop it. When she landed upside down, she had to wait upside down with her tail in the air for thirteen minutes.

After surviving this harrowing journey, the media dubbed her Felix after the cartoon cat, and her name was later adapted to the female version: Félicette. Despite the national pride the country's "astrocat" inspired, Félicette was put down two months later. The scientist wanted to study her brain.

While Félicette was forgotten about and unmentioned for a long time after her voyage, a crowdfunding campaign in 2017 raised enough money for a bronze statue to be raised for her contribution to science and the invaluable data that was collected during her space flight. The statue was unveiled on December 18, 2019, at the International Space University, where she stands five feet tall.

Interesting Fact: Despite her five-foot statue, in real life Félicette was a petite 5.5 lbs.

[22]
MRS. CHIPPY

In 1914, Sir Ernest Shackleton started his expedition to the Antarctic. On his ship, *Endurance*. there was a remarkable cat by the name of Mrs. Chippy.

Mrs. Chippy belonged to the ship's carpenter, Harry "Chippy" McNish, and managed to get the name because she followed him around like a hovering wife. Shockingly, it was later discovered that Mrs. Chippy was a boy, but the name stuck.

While on the ship, Mrs. Chippy was often seen running on the narrow rails no matter how rough the seas became. His unique personality made all the crew fall in love with him. Although Mrs. Chippy adapted to ship life very well, there were occasional problems.

A diary entry from one of the crew members talks about the cat jumping overboard, saved by the night watchman who turned the ship around. Mrs. Chippy had to be fished out using a specimen net.

Unfortunately, the ill-fated expedition got stuck in ice and the ship was destroyed. Without the ship, Shackleton decided that the animal wouldn't survive and had Mrs. Chippy and four dogs onboard shot. McNish never forgave him.

Mrs. Chippy has been featured in several books, on a stamp, in a mini-series, in paintings, and even a children's book. There is even a statue that was added to McNish's grave in 2004 to honor the beloved cat and his carpenter.

Interesting Fact: Mrs. Chippy has an opera for children called *Shackleton's Cat*.

[23]
TRIM

There are some cats that stand out for their outstanding accomplishments in history. One of them is Trim, born in the Indian Ocean on the *HMS Reliance* during its journey from the Cape of Good Hope to Botany Bay.

Shockingly enough, Trim fell overboard when he was young but managed to swim to a rope and climb up. This heroic survival effort made him a crew hero and particular favorite of Captain Matthew Flinders.

Flinders named the little kitten Trim after the butler from the novel Tristram Shandy, due to his loyalty and the great affection he showed for Flinders. Trim went on to sail with Flinders on another ship, the *HMS Investigator*, as they went around the Australian mainland. He was by Flinders' side through many perilous adventures, including a shipwreck in 1803 on the ship *HMS Porpoise* when it ran aground on Wreck Reef.

Trim was a bicolor cat, who was mainly black with white paws and a white chest. Flinders described him as having a robe of clear jet-black hair and feet that had been dipped in snow. Unfortunately, Flinders was accused of being a spy and imprisoned by the French. While Trim and Flinders were imprisoned, Trim went missing and, after two weeks, was presumed dead. It was assumed that someone had taken Trim because they were starving.

Flinders went on to write a book about Trim called *Trim: The Cartographer's Cat* in 1809, and another book was written in 2019 titled *A Cat Called Trim*. Trim's memory also lives on in a statue in Sydney with a plaque that reads:

TO THE MEMORY OF
TRIM
The best and most illustrious of his race
The most affectionate of friends,
faithful of servants,
and best of creatures
He made the tour of the globe, and a voyage to Australia,
which he circumnavigated, and was ever the
delight and pleasure of his fellow voyagers
Written by Matthew Flinders in memory of his cat
Memorial donated by the North Shore Historical Society

There are several statues of Trim and Flinders, including two more in Australia and two more in England. There aren't many cats that can claim to have had the impact that Trim did on the history books.

Interesting Fact: Since Trim was raised with sailors and spent little time around other cats, which caused him to grow up with abnormal mannerisms for a cat.

[24]
WILLOW

It's common knowledge that cats like to roam, but how far can a cat roam when they want an adventure? Well, Willow the calico cat traveled 1,600 miles on her adventure.

Willow's family, the Squires, lived in Broomfield, Colorado where she went missing in 2006 when a contractor left a door to the house open. Willow quickly made her escape, and in hopes of finding her, the Squires put up posters and messages online. Willow was two at the time and on the smaller side. Due to their location, the family sadly concluded that Willow must have been eaten by a coyote.

However, in September 2011, a good Samaritan brought Willow into Animal Control and Rescue in New York after she was found on 20th Street. Thankfully, the Squires family had a microchip implanted so the shelter was able to locate her missing family five years later.

No one knows what happened to Willow during her missing five years, but when she was reunited with her family, she had put on weight and seemed well cared for.

Interesting Fact: There was a tip to a news outlet that a man on a ski trip fell in love with Willow and brought her home to NY with him.

CHAPTER FOUR: WORKING CATS

[25]
BLACKIE

While not considered the wealthiest cat in the world anymore, Blackie still inherited enough money to put him near the top of the list. A rich British man Ben Rea died in 1988 and left most of his estate to Blackie, his cat. That inheritance was almost $13 million and in today's time, that amount would be worth $32 million. Rea made his many millions by buying and selling antiques, and he spent his hard-earned money making sure that his cats lived their best lives.

Blackie was the last of 15 cats who shared the mansion in Dorney with Ben. Although he had a human family, he wasn't close to them and didn't want them in his will. Without family to leave the money to, Rea left it to three cat charities on the condition that they take care of Blackie until his final days. Rea obviously had people he cared for in addition to the cat, because he also left money to his gardener and his mechanic.

Ben's sister, Dorothy, whom he might have been close to, died just a few days before Rea and left all her money to charities for animals as well, about $5 million in total. It seemed to be a family trait to love and care for animals.

No one knew what happened to Blackie after the money was dispersed, but it's clear that someone used the money to take care of him until he passed away.

Interesting Fact: Blackie is named for his solid black coat.

[26]
D-O-G (DEE-OH-JEE)

Named after canines, D-O-G may think he is one, particularly in light of the fact that he spends his time with over 20 dog friends every day. In St. Louis, Missouri at Support Dogs, Inc., D-O-G works as a training tool to help the dogs during their two-year training program. The program trains dogs and finds owners for them, free of charge. The dogs also work in the courtrooms with children in need of comfort. To get them ready for these very important tasks, D-O-G helps the dogs get used to other animals, teaching them to be friends with cats.

When he is not assisting in training, D-O-G spends his time establishing dominance. He can be found sleeping on the dog's beds or eating out of their bowls. D-O-G also likes to play with the dogs, batting at their noses and pulling their tails. When he is done, he snuggles up to them for a nap.

D-O-G is notorious for rearranging things in the office overnight and has earned love from the staff and many other visiting people who didn't think they were cat people.

Interesting Fact: D-O-G has a five-foot-tall condo in the middle of the office.

[27]
FRED THE UNDERCOVER KITTY

The New York Police Department isn't shy about the lengths they'll go to catch criminals, and Fred the Undercover Kitty proves it. Fred was born sometime in the spring of 2005, and he was fortunately rescued by Animal Care and Control just in time. Suffering from a collapsed lung and pneumonia, Fred wouldn't have made it much longer on the streets. Carol Moran, the assistant district attorney, decided to adopt him and bring him back to health. She also adopted his brother and named the pair Fred and George after the Weasley twins from the *Harry Potter* series.

In 2006, Fred was brought in to go undercover and pose as a patient for Steven Vassall, a man who was acting as a vet but who lacked the license and training for the job. He worked with Stephanie Green-Jones, an undercover agent, and on February 3, 2006, the duo was able to catch Vassall. He would go on to be charged with criminal mischief, petty larceny, unauthorized veterinary practice, and injuring animals. He pled guilty and was put on probation with mandatory psychiatric treatment.

From there, Fred started training as a therapy cat so that he could join the district attorney's office's program to go into schools and let children learn how to care for and treat animals. There were also talks of animal talent agencies interested in casting him in commercials. Fred's impact on the world was cut short when he escaped his home in August 2006 and was hit by a car, ending his life.

Interesting Fact: Fred received the Mayor's Alliance Award for remarkable animals.

[28]
OSCAR

Cats can map new lands, fly to space, and solve murders, but what else can they do? Oscar the cat had the eerie ability to predict death.

One of six kittens adopted by the Steere House Nursing and Rehabilitation Center located in Providence, Rhode Island, it quickly became obvious Oscar wasn't your typical cat.

Oscar was adopted to work as a therapy cat at the nursing home, which was known for being pet friendly. There are 41 beds available, and the home caters to end-stage diseases like Alzheimer's, Parkinson's, and other diseases. Despite being a therapy cat, Oscar was not friendly and hissed at people when they tried to bother him, preferring to be left alone.

But after a few months, employees noticed that Oscar would go nap on or beside the pillows of certain people. Those people would inevitably pass away within the next two hours.

At first, everyone was skeptical since there was no way that Oscar could predict who would be passing away. However, after correctly predicting 25 deaths the staff started heeding his warnings. The extra warning time made it possible for families to gather and be with their loved ones when their journey was over.

Oscar became famous in 2007 when the *New England Journal of Medicine* received a submission from a doctor at the Steere House, Dr. David Dosa. In the article, Dr. Dosa explained that he thought Oscar could detect chemicals that the body was releasing as the body started shutting down.

After many years of predicting death, Oscar the therapy cat fell ill and passed away on February 22, 2022, at 17 years old. While he might be gone, he won't be forgotten by all the families he gifted those final minutes to.

Interesting Fact: It was guessed that by 2015 alone, Oscar had predicted over 100 deaths.

[29]
SNOWBALL

It turns out that cats can put criminals behind bars too. In 1994, a woman named Shirley Ann Duguay, just 32 years old and the mother of five, went missing. Her car was discovered on Highway 169 in a rural area on Prince Edward Island, with no license plates and blood splatters throughout the car's interior.

It wasn't until May 6, 1995, that Ms. Duguay's body was discovered buried in a shallow grave where she'd been thrown after being strangled to death. Along with her body, a leather jacket was found in a bag nearby covered in her blood and strands of white feline hair.

The investigators remembered there had been a white cat named Snowball who belonged to her estranged boyfriend—their primary suspect despite the lack of evidence. The constables attempted to have the hair tested but the lab refused, saying they only tested animal hair.

Following a hunch, the lead Constable Savoie with the Royal Canadian Mounted Police found a doctor willing to test the hair at the National Cancer Institute laboratory. The doctor came up with a technique that had never been used before: a way to match a cat's DNA from a blood sample and the DNA from the hairs to see if they were a match.

Following instructions to collect the blood sample perfectly and hand deliver it to the laboratory, the Constable and doctor worked together and conducted trials to make sure their plan would work.

Over 20 cats were tested to make sure that the test worked and was proven to be fail-proof. There was one in a 45 million chance that a cat would have DNA similar to Snowballs.

The ex-boyfriend Roger Beamish was arrested, and the evidence was used against him in court where he was sentenced to 18 years in prison. Snowball was the first animal to ever get a criminal convicted.

Interesting Fact: The attorney for the defense was quoted as saying, "Without the cat, the case falls flat."

[30]
TAMA

Tama is well known in Japan for her faithful service to Kishi Station and her friendly demeanor. Tama was a female calico cat that became well-known as a station master. Though she was born a stray, she stayed close to the station because she was fed regularly by passengers. In 2004, the station was getting ready to close due to financial issues, and it was around this time that Toshiko Koyama adopted the stray calico.

Public outrage led to the station remaining open until 2006, when Wakayama Electric Railway took over. However, the new owners planned to kick all of the stray cats out of the shelter they used in the station. Koyama begged for the cats to be let into the station so that they wouldn't be without shelter, and it was decided that the cats would continue to make Kishi Station their home.

In 2007, Tama was awarded the title of station master and given a special hat that took 6 months to make just for her. Her job was to greet the passengers and she got paid in cat food. The number of passengers immediately started going up as people clamored to meet Tama the station master cat. She did so well that she won the "Top Station Runner Award" in 2007.

The next year, Tama was promoted to "superstation master," making her the sole female manager in the company. After that, she was knighted by the prefectural governor because of her positive impact on tourism in the area. She continued to be promoted to operating office, and a train was painted with pictures of her.

Tama continued to be a fixture in the company and drew crowds until her death at the age of 16 in 2015. People came from all over to her funeral, where she was given her final promotion to "honorary eternal stationmaster."

Interesting Fact: Every year on the anniversary of her death, the successor cats and the president of the company present offerings to her shrine.

[31]
UNSINKABLE SAM

A maritime hero, Unsinkable Sam, otherwise known as Oscar, was a cat that served during WWII and managed to make it out of three ship sinkings alive.

Oscar was a black and white cat who belonged to a crew member aboard the German battleship, *Bismarck*. The *Bismarck* only went on one mission, Operation Rheinübung, with the goal of blocking Allied routes to the United Kingdom. The Battle of Denmark Strait ensued, and the *Bismarck* managed to sink another ship but was heavily damaged. The ship later sank, taking all but 115 crew members out of the 2,100. Amazingly, Oscar survived and was picked up by the British ship the *Cossack*, which is where he got the name Oscar.

Oscar spent the next several months on the *Cossack* sailing the Mediterranean Sea. In October 1941, the ship was severely damaged by a torpedo from a German sub that blew off a third of the front of the boat, killing 159 crewmembers. Oscar managed to survive the attack, and after the ship sank, he moved to the aircraft carrier *Ark Royal*.

After surviving both of those ship sinkings, Oscar got the nickname "Unsinkable Sam." In November, the carrier was hit by another torpedo and started to sink slowly. All but one crew member made it off this time, and Unsinkable Sam was found hanging onto a board.

After all of his daring adventures, Unsinkable Sam lived with the Mayor of Gibraltar until he could make it back to the United Kingdom. Once back in the United Kingdom, he went to live at a home for sailors until he passed away in 1955.

Interesting Fact: Oscar the cat started out with the Axis side and switched to the Allies.

CHAPTER FIVE: ACTING CATS

[32]
DEMETER

Another famous cat from the musical *Cats* is Demeter. She is one of the main characters and a lead singer in the show. Demeter is portrayed as an extremely paranoid cat, and it is alluded to that she is that way because of traumatic events in her past.

Demeter is easily frightened or surprised, and constantly scared that Macavity will show up. She isn't a strong cat and relies on other people for emotional and moral support. One of her closest allies is Bombalurina.

From the start, Demeter is the only one who sympathizes with Grizabella the Glamour Cat. However, when forced to handle difficult situations, she runs to Bombalurina. Demeter is one of the main singers in several songs like "The Old Gumbie Cat," "Grizabella the Glamour Cat," "Macavity the Mystery Cat," and "The Jellicle Ball."

Interesting Fact: Her name comes from the Greek goddess Demeter, who is the goddess of agriculture.

[33]
GOOSE

Goose first appeared in the Marvel franchise in the movie *Captain Marvel*. A Flerken is an alien that looks just like an Earth cat, and it's easy to confuse the two. However, there are some abilities that Flerkens have that cats don't. One of the biggest differences is that they have tentacles which shoot from their mouth whenever they need to capture prey. Flerkens can keep entire dimensions in their mouth, an ability that allows them to store and teleport things, shapeshift, and eat items ten times larger than they are. Flerkens can live up to 19 years and lay hundreds of eggs at once.

Originally, Goose belonged to Mar-Vell, a scientist who came to Earth under the alias Doctor Wendy Lawson. Mar-vell was part of the Kree Empire, but defects from the Kree Empire, becoming the first Captain Marvel. After Mar-Vell dies, Goose meets Carol Danvers and S.H.I.E.L.D. She helps Danvers and Fury travel across the universe to find Mar-Vell's old lab. He helps defeat the bad guy, Yon-Rogg, and goes on to later eat the Tesseract to protect it.

One key interaction between Fury and Goose occurs when Fury tries to hold Goose, who promptly scratches his eye. Since the claws of a Flerken can sometimes carry infection, Fury ends up losing his eye. Despite this, the two make up and Goose is shown throwing up the Tesseract in Fury's office, where he continues to live until he disappears in 2009. Danvers then shows up and the two go back on travels across space.

Interesting Fact: Several cats played Goose in the movie. The main cat was Reggie and his stunt doubles were Gonzo, Rizzo, and Archie.

[34]
JONESY

Famous for his role as a space-faring cat, Jonesy is a character in the 1979 film *Alien*. Jonesy is Ellen Ripley's pet aboard the USCSS

Nostromo. His real name is Jones, but he is affectionately called Jonesy by the crew whom he helps relax.

The USCSS (United States Cargo StarShip) Nostromo, where Jones resides, was a commercial towing vehicle operated by a small crew. Its main job was to tow an automated refinery between Thedus (a mining world) and Earth. The original people who started on the Nostromo were Arthur Dallas, the Captain, executive officer Thomas Kane, navigation officer Joan Lambert, science officer Ash, chief engineer Dennis Parker, engineering technician Samuel Brett, and Ellen Ripley, warrant officer and Jonesy's owner.

The crew was placed in stasis for the long journey but was awakened early because of a distress signal coming from a planetoid. They land to investigate, and Kane becomes impregnated by a local creature. Once the creature grows up, it starts killing the entire crew. In the movie, Jonesy is woken up with everyone else, and while the crew is hunting for the creature on the ship, he accidentally sets off motion sensors making them think the creature is there. Brett goes to get Jonesy and, while trying to coax him out, Brett fails to notice the cat's hissing at the creature behind him. Brett is immediately killed. Jonesy survives because the creature has little interest in him.

In an effort to defeat the creature, the crew decides to self-destruct the ship. However, the creature manages to kill everyone except Ripley and Jonesy. They managed to blow up the ship and get to a shuttle where they remained in cryosleep for 57 years until they are eventually found. The rescue crew almost didn't help them because they were confused by the combined DNA, but finally realized the woman and the cat were two different beings.

The two went on to live in an apartment on a space station, until Ripley decided to take a job that took her off-ship. She left Jonesy behind to save him from any more trauma, and from there, we don't know what happens to the space cat.

Jonesy has appeared in many pop culture references since the film, including a sequel, *World of Warcraft*, *Halo*, a graphic novel about Jonesy, *Fortnite*, and most recently in the game *Dead by Daylight* (2023).

Interesting Fact: Since Jonesy was in cryosleep for so long, he is considered the longest-living cat.

[35]
MORRIS

Born in Chicago in 1961, Morris was a large stray orange tabby cat. Luckily for him, he didn't remain on the streets. Morris was adopted in 1968 by animal trainer Bob Martwick who took him to the audition to be the new "spokes cat" of 9 Lives cat food. Morris gave such an impressive performance that the art director was heard saying, "He's the Clark Gable of Cats."

Morris was known as the world's most finicky cat, only eating 9 Lives and nothing else. He made over 58 TV commercials from 1969 to 1978, and his acting was so good that he was awarded two PATSY Awards.

After the original Morris passed away in July 1978 of old age, similar-looking cats took his place and name. These other Morris cats became so famous that in 1988, one of them even ran for president!

Interesting Fact: The original Morris, inspiration for one of the most famous brand images in pet food history, was adopted for only $5.

[36]
MR. BIGGLESWORTH

While most cats seem to be good guys, sometimes their owners are the bad guys, like the evil stepmother in *Cinderella* or the sorcerer Gargamel in *The Smurfs*. In the *Austin Powers* franchise, Mr. Bigglesworth is a long-haired Persian cat who belongs to Dr. Evil.

In the movie, after Dr. Evil fails to kill his nemesis Austin Powers, Dr. Evil has both him and his cat cryogenically frozen for thirty years. However, something goes horribly wrong for Mr. Bigglesworth during the thawing-out procedure, and he permanently loses all his fur. A hairless sphynx by the name of Ted Nude Gent was then introduced to play Mr. Bigglesworth.

Ted Nude Gent was thought of as a pioneer in the cinematic world because of the complexity of the role he was assigned. Previously, it was thought that only a dog could play such a complex role, but Ted Nude Gent changed the game by following training that no other cat had followed before.

Sphynx cats are hairless because of a genetic mutation, but they were purposely bred starting in 1975 when a farm cat was born bald. Through selective breeding, the sphynx breed was created.

Their personalities make them great pets and cuddlers, and they are known for being one of the more intelligent cat breeds. The have plenty of energy, they're extremely social, mischievous, and highly motivated by food. As a breed, Sphinxes are pretty healthy, but because of their hairless state, they are prone to sunburn and their kittens need to be watched for respiratory problems.

Interesting Fact: Mr. Bigglesworth was created as a parody of villains from the *James Bond* franchise, who often had the same animals.

[37]
MR. JINX

In the well-known movies, *Meet the Parents* and *Meet the Fockers*, the feline star Mr. Jinx added a comedic edge to an already funny movie. In truth, the character was played by multiple cats, Bailey and Meesha. They were five years old and had such great personalities they bonded with the cast. Robert DeNiro liked Mr. Jinx so much that he insisted they be in more scenes than were originally planned.

Mr. Jinx's most famous scenes included a scene where Greg let the cat outside and eventually chased it up onto the roof. In all of the scenes, animal welfare was taken seriously, and this one was no exception. The cat had a harness attached the entire time they were off the ground.

In another scene, it appears that an urn full of Grandma's ashes is knocked over, causing Mr. Jinx to run to the pile of ashes and promptly treat it like a litter box. The trainers hid a bag of food in the ashes so that the acting cat would run over and start digging. Then, a hose ran water up to make it look like Mr. Jinx had done the unthinkable. Throughout the movie, both cats demonstrated their superior training and hilarious timing.

Interesting Fact: In the scene where the wedding dress is destroyed, a dog was placed inside the dress to move it around because the cats weren't big enough.

[38]
SASSY

Disney has a long history of starring cats in their films, both animated and live action. *Homeward Bound* is one such live action film that stars Sassy as one of the protagonists. She's a Himalayan cat with the traditional bright blue eyes and is shown as being an intelligent cat. Sassy is extremely fluffy with cream-colored fur, darker points on her ears, paws, tail, and a mask on her face.

Sassy belongs to Hope Seaver and, along with two other pets, travels cross-country to return to their home and family. The other two pets are Shadow, a wise and elderly golden retriever, and Chance, a hyper American bulldog puppy who came from a shelter. Sassy doesn't get along well with Chance to start with, but they grow closer throughout the movie as they make the journey together. Even from the start, it's obvious that Sassy and Shadow have a much closer relationship.

One of the most suspenseful moments in the movie is when the trio is trying to cross a raging river and Sassy is swept away. Shadow tries to save her, but she goes over a waterfall and appears to die. Thankfully, a man named Quentin finds her and nurses her back to health and she finds her "boys" again.

Despite facing bears, porcupines, and a mountain lion, the animal trio manages to survive and prevail, ultimately returning home to their people. Sassy portrays all of the best characteristics of a Himalayan in the movie: loyal, extremely smart, gentle, and affectionate.

Interesting Fact: Sassy was played by three different cats in the movie.

[39]
THACKERAY BINX

Hocus Pocus, a Halloween favorite and a pop culture icon from 1993, focuses on three sisters who are witches brought back to life by the lighting of the black flame candle. In the movie, the legend goes that if a virgin lights the candle on Halloween night during a full moon, the Sanderson Sisters, will return from the grave.

In the movie, there is a boy named Binx from 1693 who has a little sister Emily. Emily was taken by the Sanderson sisters and Binx tried to save her, but he was unsuccessful. Binx then insulted one of the witches. Infuriated, the Sanderson sisters cursed him and turned him into a black cat who is immortal. The sisters are then hanged by the people of Salem. Binx spends the next 300 years trying to keep anyone from bringing the sisters back—and manages to do it—until Max (one of the main characters) lights the candle.

In the movie, Binx was actually played by eight real cats all trained to perform different parts and tricks. The eight cats who were used were named Stimpy, Clyde, Killer, Felix, Rio, Mad Cat, Tom-Cat, and 'Fraidy Cat. The appearance of the cats talking was created with animatronic cats and CGI. At the end of the movie, when Binx is turned back into a boy, he is played by Sean Murray.

Interesting Fact: Jason Marsden was chosen to voice Binx because of his accent. The director wanted Binx to sound like he came from the original time of the Sanderson sisters.

[40]
TONTO

While most cats in cinematic roles are supporting actors, there is one who is the co-star of the film. In the 1974 film *Harry and Tonto*, the cat Tonto plays one of the most important roles.

Harry is a retired schoolteacher who has lived in the same New York apartment for most of his adult life. Unfortunately, his building is getting torn down to make room for a parking lot, which leaves Harry and Tonto facing an uncertain future. The dynamic duo originally goes to stay with Harry's oldest son Burt and his family.

However, after deciding that they didn't want to remain with his family, Harry and Tonto pack up to travel cross country and get dropped off at the airport. After realizing that Tonto will have to go through an X-ray machine, Harry decides to take a bus instead.

The bus ride goes well until Tonto has to go to the bathroom and Harry realizes that he won't use the toilet. After getting off the bus, Tonto runs off and the bus abandons the duo in the middle of nowhere. Not to be discouraged, Harry and Tonto buy a 1955 Chevrolet Bel Air, and even though his driver's license is expired, Harry jets off to visit his daughter in Chicago where she owns a bookstore.

During this adventure, Harry and Tonto meet many interesting people, like a hitchhiker who quotes the Bible and an underage runaway, Ginger. They finally make it to Chicago, where his daughter and grandson live. Eventually, Harry's grandson and Ginger run away to a commune and Tonto is once again his only companion.

Deciding to go further west, the pair get a ride with a health food salesman, make friends with a hooker, and spend the night in a jail with a Native American, Chief Dan George.

In the movie, Tonto is a ginger tabby with extensive leash-training, one of the reasons he is such a manageable travel companion. The idea to make Tonto a trained cat came from the director's mother, who used to walk her cat around the village on a leash. The film staff encouraged Tonto to move around the set as necessary by hiding pieces of liver for him to find. While the actor who played Harry, Art Carney, didn't care for cats, he grew to love the two feline actors who played Tonto in the movie.

Interesting Fact: Art Carney won the Oscar for Best Actor that year, and in 1975, Tonto won the PATSY, Performing Animal Top Star of the Year.

CHAPTER SIX: CARTOON CATS

[41]
BERLIOZ, TOULOUSE, AND MARIE

Duchess and O'Malley's three kittens were Berlioz, Toulouse, and Marie, the sweet and charming kittens who helped catapult *The Aristocats* to cinema fame.

Berlioz has bright blue eyes and dark fur in a deep gray. Similar to his siblings, he wears a red ribbon around his neck that often comes untied when he plays. He is the quietest of the three kittens and is easily annoyed. Out of the three, he is the most likely to have an attitude about something new or something that he doesn't like, but despite this he is just as sweet and naive as the other kittens. Beriloz's hobby is playing the piano, a skill he often showcases beautifully for his family.

Toulouse is a fluffy, orange kitten with green eyes. He is decked out with a blue ribbon tied like a bow tie. It's thought that he is the oldest of the three kittens and tries to be the defender of the family. When Toulouse acts tough, he puffs up and hisses at whoever threatens him; otherwise, he is just a friendly and laid-back kitten, the most playful of the three. His artistic interest is painting, and he practices daily to become a great master. In fact, he is the kitten who looks most like his stepfather, Thomas O'Malley.

Marie is the only girl and the middle kitten. She is a little spoiled because she believes she is all grown up just like her mother. She often acts prissy and is quick to tattle on the boys if she doesn't get her way. Similar to her mother, Marie looks like a purebred

Turkish Angora with long white fur and bright blue eyes, a pink nose, and pink paws. A daydreamer, Marie often gets caught up in romantic thoughts and sighs heavily, which leads her to pay less attention than she should. Her lack of attention leads her to be in danger constantly throughout the film, but she is saved every time.

Interesting Fact: The kittens were named after famous French people and places. Marie was named after the illustrious Marie Antoinette, Toulouse was named after a famous French painter, Henri Toulouse-Lautrec, and Berloiz shares a name with the well-known composer, Hector Berlioz.

[42]
CATBUS

In the movie, *My Neighbor Totoro*, one of the most iconic characters is a creature called Catbus. The movie was originally released in 1988 by Studio Ghibli, and an English-dubbed version was produced by Streamline Pictures in 1989. It was released in the United States in 1993.

Catbus is depicted as a large, twelve-legged creature who has a cat's head with eyes, a nose, and a feline smile. He also has a furry bus-shaped body and a large cat tail. His eyes work as headlights with windows along the side.

His job is to take spirits, like the main character Totoro, to a destination of their choosing. Catbus plays an important part in the movie because when Mei goes missing, Totoro gets Catbus to go find her and bring Satsuki to her.

Catbus was loosely based on the Cheshire Cat from *Alice in Wonderland*, as evidenced in the large "Cheshire" grin that he shows off. He is also based on a Japanese bakeneko, which is an old legend that says when a cat grows old enough, they learn how to shapeshift. There have been many plush animals and other merchandise based on Catbus.

Interesting Fact: There is a sequel *Mei and the Kittenbus* where Kittenbus is assumed to be Catbus's child.

[43]
DUCHESS

One fabulous and well-known cartoon kitty is Duchess from *The Aristocats*, a 1970 animated film. In the movie, she was voiced by several famous voice artists in every appearance she made. In the original movies, she is voiced by Eva Gabor, who also voiced Miss Bianca from all of *The Rescuers* movies. Her singing was performed by Robie Lester, one of the most sought-after voice actors in the 1960s. Later, when Duchess appeared in the *House of Mouse*, she was played by the same voice actor who was the voice of Minnie Mouse, Russi Taylor.

The elegant cat is shown as a white Turkish Angora with blue eyes and long, pure white hair. Duchess is shown to be extremely elegant, a great beauty, and the epitome of ladyship. Her owner is an aristocrat, and Duchess is the perfect cat for Madame Adelaide Bonfamille. She is also a wonderful mother to her three kittens Marie, Berlioz, and Toulouse, and is shown as patient and loving.

As a musical expert, she teaches her children to love the arts, like piano playing, singing, and painting.

Duchess doesn't like conflict and encourages her children not to fight. Her gracious, kind attitude extends to other animals and even strangers without concern for where they come from. The family lives with their owner, a former opera singer, in a large mansion where they wear gold and jewel-studded collars and have meals prepared for them by a chef.

The movie takes a turn when their owner, Madame Bonfamille, invites an old friend and lawyer, Georges Hautecourt, to the house. The two decide to discuss business and it is revealed that the cats are to inherit Madame Bonfamille's vast fortune to ensure they are well taken care of after her death. At this time a new main character is introduced: the butler, Edgar.

Edgar starts off as a sophisticated and professional butler who seems polite and loyal to the family, but after eavesdropping on the conversation between Madame Bonfamille and Hautecourt, he finds out about the cats' inheritance. In the same conversation, Edgar learns that he is next in line to inherit Madame's fortune when the cats have passed away. After doing the math and realizing that the cats could live for a very long time, he decides he doesn't want to wait and begins plotting against the cats' demise.

Edgar brings Duchess and her kittens their nightly milk, but this time it is drugged using sleeping pills to put them to sleep. Since Duchess is so gracious, she invites the family friend Roquefort, a small house mouse, to share the cats' supper. As a result, Roquefort gets drugged as well. Once the cats are asleep, Edgar gathers them up into a basket and takes him on his scooter to the countryside where he dumps them. He believed that if Madame thought the cats had run away, she'd leave the entire inheritance to him instead.

Duchess and the kittens spend the night in bad weather and have no idea where they are. Once they wake up the next morning, the feline family meets an unlikely hero, Thomas O'Malley.

Interesting fact: Duchess is the first single parent to be one of the stars of a Disney movie.

[44]
FIGARO

Figaro is a Disney animated film star appearing in the 1940's film *Pinocchio*. In the movie, he belongs to Geppetto and Pinocchio. Many of the characters in *Pinocchio* went on to become well-known in their own right, and Figaro is no exception.

Figaro was a small black and white tuxedo cat with a mischievous and rascally personality, which was based on a young and immature little boy. While Figaro has a quick temper, he also has a heart of gold. He was so popular in the movie that he went on to appear in many shorts and cartoons, mainly as Minnie Mouse's cat. In most of his appearances, he is a heroic little kitty.

Figaro the cat appeared in *Classics Disney Shorts*, *House of Mouse*, *Mickey Mouse Clubhouse*, *Mickey and the Roadster Racers*, and *Mickey Mouse Funhouse*. He was one of Walt Disney's favorite characters and he made sure to bring him back whenever the opportunity arose.

Figaro can be found in many places throughout Disney World, such as in murals telling the story of Pinocchio. Figaro has also inspired the name of the fries at Pinocchio Village Haus, called Figaro Fries. He can also be seen playing on the flower bed balcony at the restaurant.

Throughout the cartoons, Figaro expresses a lot of personality, exhibiting a strong dislike for long waits, taking a bath, being made to look foolish, and having to deal with dogs.

Interesting Fact: In a storyboard that was uncovered after *Pinocchio* was released, Figaro was originally going to be a giant cat in *Mickey and the Beanstalk*.

[45]
JIJI

Kiki's Delivery Service is an animated fantasy film released in 1989 that was produced, directed, and written by Hayao Miyazaki. In the movie, Kiki moves with her cat Jiji, a solid black cat with yellow eyes and big ears, to a small seaside town. Her village has a tradition for witches still in training to spend a year alone. Kiki and Jiji become important members of the town.

Jiji is a talking cat, probably a Cornish Rex, who acts as both a character for Kiki to take care of and a guardian and companion to Kiki. Jiji can talk to Kiki, but only does so when she isn't in front of other people. At one point, Kiki loses her magic because she gets sick and can't communicate with Jiji anymore. It's unclear at the end of the movie whether they can communicate anymore or not. Jiji represents Kiki's childlike nature, which is something she must eventually outgrow. This coming-of-age story and Jiji's role in it is captured by the word "Ji," which means "wise" in Chinese. Jiji is an important part of *Kiki's Delivery Service*, adding humor and sarcasm to the movie.

Interesting Fact: Jiji is 13 years old, which is considered an old age for a normal cat. However, because Jiji is a witch's cat, he will live longer.

[46]
LUCIFER

While Cinderella was busy losing her glass slipper, there was another well-known character who was probably busy napping. Lucifer is the cat from *Cinderella* who belongs to the evil stepmother, Lady Tremaine. He originally appeared in the 1950's animated film *Cinderella*.

Lucifer is a cunning and manipulative cat who is always scheming and finding ways to make life more difficult for Cinderella. While he is often shown as being manipulative and plotting his next act, he also spends a lot of time being lazy, napping, and overeating. Lucifer is especially fond of milk and will get quite daring to get his paws on some.

Due to his loyalty to Lady Tremaine, Lucifer is a formidable opponent to Cinderella's animal friends. The mice are often seen hiding from Lucifer, although they always manage to thwart him. When he isn't napping, he spends his time eavesdropping and gaining information that he can use to his advantage. Lucifer also employs his charm and cunning to get his way and thwart Cinderella.

Lucifer plays an important role in the story since he is always trying to get Cinderella in trouble and cause her grief. In one scene, Cinderella is told to give Lucifer a bath. Since he doesn't want a bath, he walks on the floors that Cinderella had just scrubbed by hand and makes dirty paw prints all over them—mostly out of spite.

Despite his evil disposition, Lucifer offers comedic relief to the story. The cat-and-mouse scene provides the audience with a laugh as they watch the critters go back and forth. The scene's creator, Ward Kimball, modeled Lucifer after his own pet cat when Walt Disney told Kimball his cat was the perfect inspiration.

Interesting Fact: Lucifer's name comes from the original name for the devil.

[47]
MR. WHISKERS

Framed as the bad guy in the Tim Burton Disney Film *Frankenweenie*, Mr. Whiskers belongs to Weird Girl. In the movie, Mr. Whiskers is a white Persian who is fused with a dead cat after an experiment goes horribly wrong. To top it off, he then becomes a vampire.

Originally, Mr. Whiskers didn't seem to be the brightest, but after he became a vampire cat, his personality drastically changed. He became louder and more destructive, refusing to listen to his owner. Although he is evil to everyone else, he doesn't attack Weird Girl due to his fond memories of her.

Interesting Fact: Mr. Whisker's death is one of the most violent to ever happen to a Disney villain.

[48]
MUFASA

Starring as one of the major leads in the animated film *The Lion King*, Mufasa was the father of Simba and the King of the Lions and Pride Rock. It is clear from the beginning of the movie that Mufasa is a respected character and a loving father. One of the first lessons he teaches Simba is about the circle of life and how important it is to live up to your responsibilities. He is a model father to Simba and a loving mate to Sarabi, Simba's mother.

Mufasa's teachings about the Circle of Life and about handling responsibilities help Simba rule as a king. His spirit remains a source of strength for all the lions.

In the sequels following *The Lion King*, Mufasa continues to impact his grandchildren, Kion and Kiara, along with the other cubs of the new generation.

Interesting Fact: Mufasa's name means "king" in the Manazoto language.

[49]
OLIVER

Another cat who starred in a Disney animated movie was the precocious kitten Oliver from the movie *Oliver and Company*. The film was released in 1988 and featured many musical numbers.

Oliver is a young orange tabby kitten with a tuft of hair that flops over his face. The movie opens with a box of kittens sitting on the side of the road and shows all the kittens getting home except for Oliver. Left to figure out how to survive on his own, Oliver meets Dodger, a dog. The two hatch a plan to help each other steal some hotdogs, but Oliver is left behind when Dodger runs off with all the food. Oliver chases him down to a houseboat where Dodger gives all the hotdogs to the dogs who live there. Oliver learns how hard it is for poor dogs to make it. Oliver then meets the dogs' owner, a criminal named Fagin who loves his animals but is broke.

Since Fagin needs money, the dogs come up with a plan to rob a limo. In the failed attempt, Oliver is caught by a little girl, Jenny, riding in the limo, who eventually takes him home. Jenny is the one who actually gives Oliver his name and takes him back to her mansion, where she proceeds to spoil and feed him. Jenny's parents are always gone, and she doesn't have anybody to spend time with, so Oliver is a much-needed companion for the young girl.

While Oliver is very happy to have found a new home, the family poodle is not at all happy to have a cat around. She helps Dodger and the other dogs kidnap Oliver. Dodger thinks he is rescuing Oliver, but doesn't realize that Oliver is happy. After Jenny also gets kidnapped and Fagin comes in to save everybody, Oliver gets to go home to his new family and Jenny finds new friends in all the dogs and Fagin.

Interesting Fact: *Oliver and Company* is the 27th animated movie Disney produced.

[50]
SI AND AM

In a movie all about dogs, Si and Am managed to make an impression. *Lady and The Tramp* was an animated film released in 1955 that focused on the complex relationships of animals.

In the movie, Lady is a Cocker Spaniel who comes from a family that spoils and pampers her. Her family, Jim Dear and Darling, make sure that Lady has never wanted for anything in her life. However, when Jim Dear and Darling have a baby, things start to change for Lady. After the baby is born, Aunt Sarah comes to stay and take care of the baby and Lady, and she brings along Si and Am, a pair of Siamese sisters known for their love of mischief.

When Si and Am come into the house, they immediately start causing problems that they then blame on Lady. While they are normally seen riding in a picnic basket that Aunt Sarah carries around, they are nothing but trouble when they come out.

In *Lady and the Tramp*, Si and Am's first big scene features them singing "The Siamese Cat Song," during which they destroy the entire house. At one point they even try to eat the family bird and the fish. Lady tries to save the fish and bird, chasing them off after they try to get to the baby's milk. A huge commotion takes place and Aunt Sarah comes rushing down to find Si and Am faking injury, thereby blaming Lady for the damage.

The book, *Lady and the Tramp*, is based on a story that appeared in 1945 *Cosmopolitan* magazine called "Happy Dan, the Cynical Dog." In the original story, the cats killed the rat and put it in the crib getting Tramp in trouble. When Tramp is sent off to be put down, they feel horrible and admit it was their fault.

Interesting Fact: The Siamese cats' original names were Nip and Tuck.

[51]
SIMBA

A big cat who stole the big screen is Simba from Disney's *The Lion King*, released in 1994. In the movie, Simba starts off as a young lion cub, son of the King of Pride Rock. Due to Simba's impulsivity and his evil uncle's scheming, Simba loses his father and runs away to escape the imagined disappointment and anger of his pride.

Simba runs into two of the other main characters, Timon and Pumbaa, who provide comic relief in the middle of a tense situation. Timon is a meerkat known for being a quick wit, funny, and loyal, and Pumbaa is a kind-hearted and exuberant warthog who formed a makeshift family of two with his best friend Timon. They rescued Simba when he ran away from his pride and introduced him to a carefree lifestyle with no responsibilities. The three stay together as Simba grows up.

Simba stays with his newfound family until he runs into Nala, a lioness from his pride who tells him how bad things have gotten with Simba's uncle in charge. Nala encourages Simba to come back to the pride and resume his responsibilities. After they defeat his uncle, with the help of Timon and Pumbaa, Nala and Simba get married and return the pride to its former glory.

Simba went on to star in several more movies, and the franchise continues to be popular to this day. The original Disney movie has also been turned into an award-winning Broadway musical, complete with stunning animal costumes and all the original musical numbers from the movie.

Interesting Fact: The name Simba was on the list of "Top 10 Trendiest Dog Names of the Year" in 2009 and again in 2013 and was the 17th most-used cat name.

[52]
THOMAS O'MALLEY

Thomas O'Malley is a smooth-talking and adventure-seeking street cat who loves his life of freedom. Thomas's full name is Abraham de Lacy Guiseppe Casey Thomas O'Malley. His names have different origins reflecting his diverse and unsettled past. Delacey is a Norman name, Giuseppe is an Italian name, Casey is an Irish name, O'Malley is Irish, Abraham is Hebrew, and Thomas is Aramaic. Phil Harris voices him in the original movie.

When Thomas first spots Duchess, he is instantly smitten by her looks and shocked when he finds out that she has three kittens. Thomas decides to help them get back to Paris, finding them a milk truck to ride on. He plans to say goodbye, but when Marie almost falls off the truck, Thomas grabs her to stop the fall, causing him to jump onto the truck with the other cats. As a result, Thomas decides to be their guide home.

Later, when the cats arrive in Paris, Thomas leads them to a friend's place to stay. At Scat Cat's place, Thomas introduces the cat family to a bunch of alley cats who all play instruments and impress Duchess and the kittens with their jazz skills. After a fun night, they return home. Duchess and the kittens meow to be let in, but they are captured by Edgar again. However, Thomas and the alley cats come to their rescue, ultimately managing to get rid of Edgar.

After saving Duchess and the kittens, Thomas marries Duchess and becomes a part of the family, deciding that a life as a housecat with a family he loves is the best life he could have.

Interesting Fact: Thomas O'Malley is the first stepfather to appear in a Disney film.

CHAPTER SEVEN: CATS ON THE TELLY

[53]
ARTEMIS

Artemis was a white cat with a crescent moon on his head just like Luna. He was sent down with Luna with a similarly limited memory, at which point he found Minako Aino and focused on training her. With Artemis's help, Minako Aino becomes Sailor V, later revealed to be Sailor Venus.

Even though he is named after Artemis, the Greek goddess of hunting, nature, and wild animals, he is not bothered by the association with the goddess, despite being teased on occasion. It's revealed that both Artemis and Luna were advisors to the queen before their kingdom was destroyed and were entrusted with the very important job of guiding the girls on Earth as they try to figure out who they are and what their mission is.

In the series, it is obvious that Artemis cares about Luna since he comforts her whenever she is sad or worried, and there are implied romantic moments between Artemis and Luna. Their relationship is confirmed when their daughter from the future is introduced.

In all the storylines of *Sailor Moon*, Artemis's core self remains the same: he is consistently loyal, an excellent advisor, and very brave. Nevertheless, in the manga series, he did tend to pitch occasional fits whenever he thought that Minako was acting irresponsibly. Similar to Luna, Artemis can transform into a human for brief moments, such as when he saved Minako from falling off a crane.

Interesting Fact: Artemis's known dislikes include being clumsy and getting into hot water with Luna.

[54]
BABBIT AND CATSTELLO

Babbit and Catstello are Warner Bros cartoons that made their appearance in three different cartoons. The cartoons were aired between 1942 and 1946. The two characters were based on the comedic duo Abbott and Costello.

Abbott and Costello were well-known comedians who could be found on the radio, on film, and on television, putting them at the top of comedic performers in the 40s and 50s. They were even the highest-paid comedians during World War II. They were so talented that their bit, "Who's on First?", is still considered one of the best ever created.

Babbitt is a tall, skinny cat and Catstello is a short fat cat. Their first appearance in "A Tale of Two Kitties" shows the two chasing a bird to eat for dinner. This bird was the precursor to Tweety, and like the Looney Toons cats, Babbitt and Catstello try and fail constantly to outwit the bird. This trope was repeated in all of Tweety's future appearances.

They next appeared in "Tale of Two Mice," but in a twist, the two appeared as mice. The focus of the cartoon was to get cheese from the kitchen fridge, but they were thwarted by the cat. After Babbit forces Catstello to go get the cheese alone, it turns out to be Swiss — Catstello's least favorite kind of cheese.

Interesting Fact: The pair have made a guest appearance in many of the Looney Toons shows, such as "The Sylvester & Tweety Mysteries."

[55]
CATDOG

In a cartoon series that was televised from 1998 to 2005 on *Nickelodeon*, there are two conjoined brothers who have to learn to deal with their unique existence—one is a cat, and one is a dog. They both have unique personalities, which leads to some hilarious problems.

Cat is the name of the cat brother, the smarter of the two. He likes to come up with plans and schemes that mostly go wrong. He is constantly trying to find ways to get fame and fortune, but unfortunately, his brother isn't concerned about that.

Of the two of them, Cat is older by minutes and makes sure to act like the older brother. Since he is smart enough to notice and understand all of the ridicule they get because of their appearance, Cat tends to be more defensive and aggressive. Despite his gruff personality, he is actually quite sophisticated, but does have a tendency to cry. With his uptight personality, he strives to keep everything clean and organized.

Interesting Fact: Even though he can drive, Cat doesn't have a driver's license.

[56]
DIANA

Diana is first introduced in *Black Moon Arc* in *Sailor Moon*, where the Sailor Guardians time travel to the 30th century to defeat the Death Phantom. Upon their return to the 20th century, Diana joins them. In the anime, she shows up in *Sailor Moon SuperS* and starts calling Artemis "father," much to Luna's shock and dismay.

Later, it is revealed that she is the daughter of Luna and Artemis and looks like a mix of her parents with gray fur and a crescent moon. She is the guardian to Chibiusa, a small child who also traveled from the 30th century to seek help from the Sailor Guardians. Chibiusa eventually trains to become a member of the Sailor Guardians with Diana by her side the whole time.

While she doesn't seem to have any special powers and is very small, Diana does help the guardians by providing knowledge from the future. Despite being timid, her bravery shines through when it needs to.

Interesting Fact: Diana is named after her father because the Roman version of Artemis is Diana.

[57]
FELIX THE CAT

Felix the Cat was a cartoon character made up by Pat Sullivan and Otto Messmer in 1919. He continues to be one of the most recognized cartoon characters in film history, portrayed as a younger black cat who has white eyes and a giant grin. His name comes from Thomas Mitchell, nicknamed Australia Felix, who was an Australian explorer.

He was first shown on November 9, 1919, in "Master Tom," an animated short that was later renamed *Feline Follies*. He is commonly accepted as the world's first animated film star, starring in the era of silent films, and eventually appearing in more and more places. He was the first giant balloon to appear in the Macy's Thanksgiving Day parade and even became the Yankees' mascot in 1922. Felix was so famous that Charles Lindbergh took a Felix doll with him on his transatlantic flight.

In all his appearances, Felix is depicted as being mischievous but with a good heart and a playful spirit. Felix is a creative problem solver with a zany side. There are other characters that appear with Felix, including his owner named Willie Jones, a mouse named Skiddoo, Felix's three nephews Inky, Dinky, and Winky, and his girlfriend Kitty. The original cast of characters changed the animated movie industry forever.

Interesting Fact: Felix the Cat has his own star on the Hollywood Walk of Fame.

[58]
HELLO KITTY

One of the most famous fictional cats is Hello Kitty, created in 1974 by Japanese company Sanrio. Working at Sanrio, Yuko Shimizu was the person who originally designed Hello Kitty and made sure that she followed the common Japanese tradition of kawaii. In

Japanese, the word "kawaii" means a combination of words like lovely, loveable, cute, and adorable. It can refer to a person or non-humans and, in this case, it was the design inspiration for Hello Kitty.

She is a white cat with a red bow over her left ear, a yellow nose, no mouth, and big cartoonish black eyes. The very first time that Hello Kitty appeared was on a vinyl coin purse in 1975 when she instantly became a huge hit, a worldwide sensation, and Sanrio's biggest asset.

Hello Kitty's given name is Kitty White, and she was born in the suburbs of London, England on November 1, 1974. Her background includes details such as her type A blood type and the fact that she is a Scorpio. Hello Kitty is a 3rd-grade student around 9 years old who has a twin sister, Mimmy, and a wonderful pet cat, Charmmy Kitty.

Some of her favorite hobbies include traveling, music, reading, eating her sister's cookies, and making new friends.

Some of her animated series include *Hello Kitty's Furry Tale Theater* (1987), *Hello Kitty and Friends* (1989–1998), *Hello Kitty's Paradise* (1999), *Growing Up with Hello Kitty* (2001), *Hello Kitty's Animation Theater* (2001), *Hello Kitty's Stump Village* (2005), and *Hello Kitty: Ringo no Mori* (2006–2008). Hello Kitty even has theme parks and attractions devoted to her character. There have been games based on Hello Kitty and her friends and family including *Super Monkey Ball*, *Mobile Legends*, *SINoALICE*, and *Kero Kero Keroppi no Boken Nikki*.

There are other characters that appear on clothing, accessories, home decor, bags, stationery, and glassware along with Hello Kitty from the franchise. Chococat is the smart cat, Kuromi is a white rabbit with a black jester's hat that has a pink skull, Pochacco is a white dog with black floppy ears, and Dear Daniel is Hello Kitty's boyfriend and childhood best friend.

Interesting Fact: Kitty's favorite fruit is apples.

[59]
JIBANYAN

Jibanyan is one of the main characters of the Japanese franchise *Yo-kai Watch*. The franchise came out with several animated series along with video games, all of which featured the spunky cat.

In the animated series, Jibanyan was originally a cat that belonged to a little girl named Amy. Amy loved him dearly, and Jibanyan still talks fondly about how many naps they took together and how much she loved him. Unfortunately, Jibanyan was hit by a car and died. Before he passed away, he was named Rudy, but after he died, he became a Yo-kai of the Charming Tribe.

Jibanyan is a red and white cat who has big yellow eyes and a tail that splits into two blue flames at the end. As a Yo-kai, he tries to avenge himself, possessing innocent people to fight the trucks that killed him because he cannot fight the trucks himself. At first, Jibanyan comes across as a rule breaker with a mischievous personality, but after almost getting exorcized and becoming friends with the other character, Nate, he settles down.

Jibanyan then spends his time making sure that Nate is safe from other Yo-kai, while also enjoying chocolate bars that he calls "choco bars" and listening to his favorite music group the "Next HarrMEOWny."

Interesting Fact: Jibanyan is based on the old folklore of a nekomata, a mythical cat with two tails originating from a domestic cat that lives too long and develops powers.

[60]
LUNA

The animated series, *Sailor Moon*, which was released in 1992, features an important feline character named Luna. Luna is the advisor to Usagi Tsukino, also known as Sailor Moon, the main character. She was the one to find Usagi's special power.

An all-black cat with a gold quarter moon on her forehead, big eyes, and big whiskers, Luna is obviously very committed to the mission. The mission starts with helping Usagi find the rest of the Sailor Guardians, especially Princess Serenity. At the beginning of the series, Luna didn't know that Usagi was the Princess Serenity or the Moon Princess.

Luna and Usagi go out and find Ami Mizuno, Sailor Mercury, Rei Hino, Sailor Mars, and Makoto Kino, Sailor Jupiter. The place that they came from, the Moon Kingdom, had fallen to the Dark Kingdom, and Luna was sent to Earth to help guide the girls who would eventually be born on Earth. Due to her devotion to Princess Serenity, part of Luna's memory was blocked so that she could do her job better.

In the series, Luna is a serious cat who is always encouraging to the girls and is almost motherly toward them. She has the ability to summon items for the Sailor Senshi by somersaulting in the air. Some of the items she summons include the Usagi Disguise Pen, the Moon Stick, Transformation Pens, and a supercomputer. In some versions of the cartoon, Luna can briefly take on a human form, but changes back if she sneezes or is startled.

Interesting Fact: Luna's name comes from the Latin word for Moon.

[61]
MEOWTH

One of the most famous Pokémon in the *Pokémon* franchise, Meowth is a Pokémon that belongs to Team Rocket members Jessie and James. The trio spends their time following Ash Ketchum around trying to steal his Pokémon, and although they would like to take any of Ash's Pokémon, they especially want Pikachu.

Unlike other Pokémon in the series, Meowth does not spend his time in a Pokéball. Instead, Meowth roams around freely with Jesse and James. He is known for his witty personality and his sarcasm, which he uses to great effect when mocking Jessie and James.

Meowth is a light brown, feline-looking Pokémon who walks on two legs and has cat ears that darken to black. He also has a gold medallion in the center of his forehead. In most episodes, Team Rocket and Meowth come up with a scheme that always backfires, and at the end of the episode they're seen being launched off to plan more dastardly deeds.

Despite being villains, it's obvious how much the three members of Team Rocket care for each other. Jesse and James really love Meowth, more than most people love their Pokémon.

Interesting Fact: The fantastical and evolved Meowth is based off of a Persian cat.

[62]
SALEM SABERHAGEN

In the 1996 TV series, *Sabrina the Teenage Witch,* a teenage witch discovers she has powers while living with her aunts. Salem, a short-haired talking black cat famous for his dry wit and hilarious one liners, lives in the home with Sabrina and her aunts.

In the series, the witches live extremely long lives, with both of Sabrina's aunts being 600 years old. Throughout the series, it is revealed that Salem is a 500-year-old witch who had attempted to take over the world and was turned into a cat for a 100-year sentence by the Witches' Council.

Salem is the only character besides Sabrina who appears in every single episode, often bringing a witty, sarcastic edge to the series. Even though he is obviously selfish, with a power-hungry mindset, he also has a soft side that comes out where Sabrina is involved because he adores her. Throughout the show, he comes up with schemes to cause trouble, take over the world, or at least get his way.

The show continued for seven seasons and eventually ended in 2003. In the last two seasons, Salem spends time at college with Sabrina and then appears at her wedding where he is dressed in a tiny tux. Everyone gets their happy ending as Sabrina runs off with the guy Salem always preferred.

Interesting Fact: In talking scenes, an animatronic cat was used.

[63]
SCRATCHY

While most people have heard of *The Simpsons*, the show features a cat star who might not be remembered as often. The *Itchy and Scratchy Show* is shown as part of the *Krusty the Clown Show* within the *Simpsons* universe. These cartoons would show up for less than a minute and were packed with violence and gore.

The two main characters of the cartoons, Itchy and Scratchy, are a mouse and black cat respectively. All of the cartoons show the two characters maiming, and in many of the shorts, killing each other. Itchy kills Scratchy in all of the shows, but there is one episode where Scratchy finally gets to kill Itchy.

The entire idea behind the shorts is to mimic classics like *Tom and Jerry*, but much more gruesomely. Scratchy first appeared in the 1928 cartoon *That Happy Cat*; it was poorly done and featured only 14 seconds of Scratchy walking, whistling, and tipping his hat. Scratchy then appeared in a cartoon with Itchy called *Steamboat Itchy*. The cartoon was made as a parody of *Steamboat Willie* by Disney. Over time, Scratchy gained popularity and appeared in more and more shorts.

Interesting Fact: A video game was released called *The Itchy & Scratchy Game* that was made for Sega/Genesis, Game Gear, Game Boy, and Super NES.

[64]
SMELLY CAT

From the beloved TV series *Friends*, there is a mention of a cat that quickly gained popularity by the name of Smelly Cat. In the TV show, Smelly Cat appears in a song about a cat that is neglected by humans because it smells so bad.

The song was part of Phoebe's character development, but it was so well-liked and popular that fans wanted an album. In 1999, the actress that played Phoebe, Lisa Kudrow, and the Pretenders recorded a version of the song and called themselves Phoebe Buffay and the Hairballs.

As a comedy song, "Smelly Cat" quickly gained popularity and has been a fan favorite since its first debut.

Interesting Fact: The song was written by Adam Chase and Betsy Borns, the writers for *Friends*.

[65]
SNARF

Snarfs are a type of reptile/cat hybrid species that hail from the TV show, *ThunderCats*. Originally. there was a whole planet of snarfs, but their planet was destroyed, leaving only 43 to find refuge on a new planet; the Planet of Snarfs. However, some of the other survivors made their way to the New Thundera, where they were freed from forced service to Mumm-Ra by the ThunderCats.

Snarfs are known for being extremely smart and capable of doing caregiving tasks, such as cooking or nursing. They have communication skills that extend to both people and animals. One of the unique characteristics of snarfs is their reptile-like tails that are prehensile and very strong. Sometimes, they stand on them much like a kangaroo. In the *ThunderCats* universe, snarfs are the only creatures who don't have any evil tendencies.

The most well-known of the snarfs is Snarf, also known as Snarf Osbert. Snarf works as a nanny or caregiver to the young Lion-O, and often considers himself the oldest of the group. He spends most of his time worrying and being pessimistic, but when called to defend Lion-O, he is as brave as any other ThunderCat.

Since Lion-O grew up, Snarf has felt like he isn't getting as much attention and that he has nothing to contribute to the group. However, as the series develops, it's clear that he still has an important role to play. He continues to mentor all the cats and remind them not to overreact.

He makes sure all of the cats are fed and takes care of the cooking, but that's not his only ability — since he is so small, Snarf fits in a lot of places and is very agile. Whenever the cats' lair is invaded or the ThunderCats are captured, it's Snarf to the rescue using his stealthy maneuvering.

Interesting Fact: Along with talking to humans and animals, Snarf can also communicate telepathically.

[66]
SNOWBALL I, II, III, IV, AND V

In the TV series *The Simpsons*, the family has a cat named Snowball, but she never made an actual appearance in the show. All of the pets on *The Simpsons* seem to come to an untimely demise, only to be replaced.

Snowball I died before the show ever started and is mentioned when Marge is writing a family Christmas letter. The first Snowball was 5 years old when she passed away and had white fur and green eyes. It's explained in a poem by Lisa that Snowball I was ran over by a Chrysler and possibly by Clovis Quimby, the Mayor's drunk brother. The cat is even depicted after death when Bart dies momentarily and goes to heaven, only to see Snowball I with tire treads on her.

Snowball II was not a white cat but inherited the name despite her black coloring. Snowball II was quite the hero on the show, once pulling Homer out of a treehouse that was on fire. Sadly, she was run over by a car as well.

The third Simpsons cat was Snowball III, who was saved from an animal shelter after the death of Snowball II. In the animal shelter, the competition wasn't too tough since Lisa had to pass over a cat with an eye infection, a skunk, a too-needy cat, and a Siamese. Snowball III was a brown cat and didn't last long in the Simpson household. When they got home, Lisa left to get food in the kitchen and Snowball III drowned in the fish tank after failing to catch the fish.

Snowball IV, known as Coltrane, was the 4th cat and adopted from the animal shelter. Despite the traumatic events of the first three cats, Lisa decided she did want another cat and was charmed by Coltrane's association with jazz player John Coltrane. In her excitement, she put on some of his music and scared Snowball IV out the window, where he fell to his death. He was the only cat besides the original to actually have white fur.

The 5th cat, Snowball V, was another black cat who looked just like Snowball II. Lisa didn't want to keep this one at first since she had such a bad track record, but after the cat leaves and narrowly avoids being hit by a car, Lisa decides to keep him. She renames him Snowball II to save money on dishes, an appropriate homage given the resemblance between the cats. Snowball V ends up staying with the Simpsons, except for a short time when she decides to live with another family, who overfeed her causing her to become overweight.

Interesting Fact: The first Snowball was most likely a Persian.

[67]
SPOT

In *Star Trek,* several animals live aboard the spaceship the U.S.S. Enterprise, including Spot, Data's American shorthair cat. While Spot acted like an average cat, constantly jumping up on things and occasionally wanting to play, she never had to worry about dogs or got a chance to chase rodents or insects. Nevertheless, Data made sure to give her plenty of attention that more than made up for her lack of prey. Spot was strictly a one-person cat and didn't have much time or attention to give to anyone other than Data, whom she adored.

In the *Star Trek* year 2370, Spot had kittens with one of the other cats living on the Enterprise at the time. Data paid close attention to Spot's health, wanting to make sure she was going to have a healthy birth. When it came time for Spot to give birth, Data and Captain Picard were away and the crew and animals were infected with a synthetic T-cell that caused them to devolve. However, Spot gave birth during the breakout, and the kittens were not affected despite their mother devolving. Data realized that the placenta protected the kittens, enabling him to make a cure and save everyone.

While Spot played an important role in the series, it is unclear what happened to her.

Interesting Fact: Spot was played by several cat actors including Monster, Zoe, Bud, Tyler, Spencer, and Brandy.

[68]
SYLVESTER

Another famous animated cat is Sylvester, or Sylvester J. Pussycat, Sr., who appears in the *Looney Tunes* and *Merrie Melodies*. He became famous and well-known for his lisp, mischievous personality, and constant pursuit of Tweety Bird, a yellow canary.

Sylvester was created by Friz Freleng and first appeared in *Life with Feathers* on March 24, 1945. His rivalry with Tweety Bird became one of the favorite parts of the *Looney Tunes* antics. Sylvester is a black and white cat with a tuxedo pattern, white chest, and white feet.

Tweety Bird is not the only character Sylvester chases. He was also known for trying to catch Speedy Gonzales, the "fastest mouse in all of Mexico" and Hippety Hopper, a young kangaroo that Sylvester mistakes for a giant mouse.

However, Sylvester somehow always winds up chasing Tweety again. He's a cunning kitty who is determined to catch Tweety no matter what. Unfortunately, Tweety is a smart bird and outsmarts Sylvester and stays out of his clutches, much like Jerry the mouse.

Sylvester speaks with a lisp and is well known for his famous catchphrase "sufferin' succotash!" Not only does Sylvester appear in the cartoons, but he also makes appearances in comic books, video games, and the live action movie *Space Jam*.

Interesting Fact: The name Sylvester comes from the scientific name for a European wildcat, Felis silvestris.

[69]
TOM

Tom is the famous cat from the cartoon *Tom and Jerry*. His full name is Thomas Jasper Cat Sr. and is portrayed as a bluish-gray shorthair cat with a tuxedo pattern. Tom's tuxedo pattern is white, as are his hands, feet, tail, mouth and belly. He is most likely meant to resemble a tuxedo British shorthair.

His first appearance was in 1940 in a short film titled *Puss Gets the Boot*. Originally his name was Jasper, but he was renamed in the second short film. The film went on to get an Oscar nomination. Tom then got his own cartoon with *Tom and Jerry*. Metro-Goldwyn-Mayer (MGM) was the company that produced *Tom and Jerry* beginning in 1940 and running until 1958, accumulating seven Academy Awards while on air.

Tom and Jerry ran again in 1961–1962 and passed by Looney Tunes as the highest-grossing animated short film. It came back for a run in 1963–1967, with even more shorts produced after 2001. In total, *Tom and Jerry* is comprised of 166 shorts, not counting all the spin-offs and movies that Tom starred in.

The entire plot of *Tom and Jerry* revolves around the fights between Tom and the mouse Jerry. Tom is constantly trying to catch Jerry in increasingly ridiculous schemes that almost always end in disaster. Jerry is cleverer and manages to stay out of Tom's clutches for the most part. However, despite their ongoing battle, they display true love and care for each other. They work together whenever they have to and save each other's lives every time they are in real danger. The only time they don't save each other is in *The Two Mouseketeers*, when Tom unfortunately loses his head to the guillotine.

One thing that made *Tom and Jerry* so popular was the fact that the writers took the "gags" to the next level, letting Tom use weapons, explosives, and poison to try and kill Jerry, an unusual display of violence for animated shorts. Even Jerry the mouse is violent, often doing real harm to Tom, but the show is nevertheless free from blood and gore.

While they don't talk much, Tom and Jerry express a lot through body language and music. The other characters in the cartoon talk whenever they appear, and Tom can frequently be found singing in attempts to woo a variety of female cats. There are several other characters like Spike and Tyke the dogs, Butch and Toodles the cats, and Nibbles the mouse.

Interesting Fact: *Tom and Jerry* is still appearing in different formats, and it entered international markets in 2022 and 2023.

[70]
TOP CAT

Originally coming out in 1961, *Top Cat* ran for 30 episodes and featured a gang of stray cats and their antics. It was only the second animated series to make it to prime time in the United States.

The main character, Top Cat, is a parody of Arnold Stang on *The Phil Silvers Show* and is voiced by Arnold Stang himself. The cats live in the grimy Hoagy's Alley and consist of the leader Top Cat, Fancy-Fancy, Brain, Choo-Choo, Spook, and Benny the Ball.

Top Cat would be considered a con man if he were human, but as a cat, he is yellow with a white muzzle and a long tail. His iconic look consists of a purple vest and a purple pork pie hat. Fancy-Fancy was always shown with a white scarf and medium brown coloring with a lighter muzzle and a black-tipped tail. Slightly shaggier, Brain was an orange cat with a purple shirt. He is portrayed as the one who can't keep a secret and handles the group's finances. Choo-Choo was a tall, pink-colored cat with a white turtleneck, a long bushy white-tipped tail, and a light muzzle. Spook was a green-tinted cat who spoke just like a beatnik or a surfer and was portrayed as a pool shark and charming rogue. Benny is the shortest member of the gang, has purple fur, and is always wearing a white jacket. He's also the right-hand man of Top Cat.

The cats are all sweet, but nevertheless are rascals who often get into trouble with a police officer, Charlie Dibble. The cats are always coming up with get-rich-quick scams, but never manage to pull them off successfully and often run into trouble in the process. To add to the chaos, Officer Dibble is usually right on their tails trying to arrest or evict them from the alley. He always tries to get them to clean the alley and follow the rules, but they don't do either.

Interesting Fact: Similar to *The Flintstones*, *Top Cat* utilized a scene technique called the "cold open," where a scene from the middle of the episode would play, followed by a flashback, and then the opening theme song.

CHAPTER EIGHT: COMIC CATS

[71]
AZRAEL

Smurfs, those famously small, blue creatures, started captivating audiences in 1958 as a comic. Part of the enduring attraction of the Smurfs is Gargamel, the evil sorcerer, and his loyal feline Azrael. The series and movies focus on the Smurfs, small blue creatures that live in mushroom houses in a secluded and peaceful forest. While most of their life is idyllic, wicked Gargamel is always trying to catch them with the help of Azrael.

Azrael's name is based off the Angel of Death in the Judeo-Christian tradition. Azrael plays an important part in the comic books, as well as the 1981 and the 2021 Smurfs show. In the comic books, Azreal was originally a female, but was later changed to a male cat.

As Gargamel's main companion, Azreal is shown to be extremely smart and understands what is being said to him. However, in true cat-like spirit, he does what he wants regardless. For example, he is shown freeing the Smurfs on occasion, simply because he is a cat. He has been portrayed as an orange cat and as a brown cat with different colored eyes, but he always goes by the same name.

While he is an evil sorcerer's cat, Azrael isn't evil himself. He has been known to team up with the Smurfs on occasion, like in the episode "Lost Cat" when he leaves Gargamel behind to live with the Smurfs.

Interesting Fact: The only time Azrael is shown as a kitten is in the episode "Gargamel's Time Trip."

[72]
GARFIELD

Created by Jim Davis in the late 70s, *Garfield* took the world by storm and hasn't stopped since. Garfield the cat is known as lazy and fat who is only interested in eating and sleeping. But it's his personality that made him famous, with his sarcastic wit and cynical opinions, along with his love of lasagna and his loathing of exercise and Mondays.

He was born June 19, 1978, in the kitchen of Mamma Leoni's Italian restaurant. Garfield loved lasagna from birth, as he quickly started to eat all the pasta in the restaurant. Since he was eating all the food, the owner had to choose between staying in business and keeping Garfield, so off to the pet store he went.

Jon Arbuckle came in and quickly adopted Garfield, although he later referred to him as a lasagna with fur and fangs. Jon also has a beagle named Odie, whom Garfield takes advantage of as the quintessential dumb dog. Odie is a beagle mix who is shown as easily excitable, happy, and despite the sometimes mean things he does to him, Garfield's best friend.

While Garfield's looks have changed over the years, he has always been an orange tabby. Over the years, he changed from being morbidly obese to just overweight. He's also become more human-like over the years, as he now walks on his back legs and has started talking.

Garfield is known for being an extremely smart cat and has no problem using a phone when he orders lasagna. In fact, he sometimes orders 50 boxes of lasagna a week. He also spends a lot of time watching TV and can use the remote and most other electronics.

Garfield doesn't talk in the comics, instead using thought bubbles to communicate. In TV adaptations, Garfield's mouth does move, but only other animals can understand what he is saying.

Along with owner Jon Arbuckle and best friend Odie, there are several other supporting characters that make *Garfield* so popular. Nermal is Garfield's opposite—cute and cuddly and annoyingly happy all the time. The pranks and jokes that Garfield plays on Nermal are part of the comedy that makes Garfield so great. Squeak is Garfield's mouse friend, and since Garfield is so lazy, he has no interest in chasing mice. This leads Garfield and Squeak to work out deals to keep the mice hidden from Jon.

Interesting Fact: While *Garfield* is one of the most well-known comic strips worldwide, the creator Jim Davis also created other comics like *Tumbleweeds*, *Gnorm Gnat*, and *Mr. Potato Head*.

[73]
HEATHCLIFF

Five years before there was Garfield, there was another orange cat storming the comic strips, Heathcliff. Called the original orange cat, Heathcliff has a very different origin story compared to the well-known Garfield.

Heathcliff was not born in a loving home, but instead was born on what would be considered "the wrong side of the tracks." Since he was born in such a rough neighborhood, he had to quickly learn to handle himself, growing up with a mean streak and the knowledge to take care of himself.

Luckily Heathcliff was not going to be left to fight it out on the streets but was instead adopted by a family named the Nutmegs. The family consisted of Grandma Nutmeg, the spoiler of the family, Grandpa Nutmeg, who butts heads with Heathcliff constantly throughout the comics, Iggy, Heathcliff's best friend and co-conspirator, Spike the Bulldog, Heathcliff's sworn enemy, and a host of neighborhood kids and supporting animal characters.

The man behind Heathcliff was George Gately, a born cartoonist. From time he was a boy, he had no doubt that he had found his life's calling. His natural talent for gag humor got him started in comics after a less-than-fulfilling career in advertising. The first comic that he launched was *Hapless Harry*, which was extremely well-liked, and Gately went on to create others like *Hippy*, *Auntie*, and *The Hintleys*.

However, it was his next comic that gained the author's attention. *Heathcliff* would become an instant success, with the character going on to star in 50 books, over 80 television shows, and one movie. Since *Heathcliff* was so popular, the franchise became the family business with John Gallagher, George Gately's brother, joining the team to help create the well-known feline. Later, their nephew, Peter Gallagher, was brought into the business. He continues to work on the *Heathcliff* comics since taking it over in 1998.

Interesting Fact: In 1974, the *Los Angeles Times* dropped the Heathcliff comics until almost 1,000 readers protested via letters. The comic would go on to make Gately a millionaire.

[74]
HOBBES

Calvin and Hobbes is a comic strip created by Bill Watterson about Calvin and his stuffed tiger, Hobbes. The comic originally ran from 1985 to 1995, and later was printed in book form. The comic strip was much beloved for its portrayal of a child's imagination and covers a range of topics from Calvin's point of view with his best bud Hobbes right beside him.

Calvin is active and imaginative just like any normal 6-year-old boy and loves to play with his stuffed tiger Hobbes. The dynamic duo gets into many adventures and misadventures, from exploring and imagining in the woods behind their house, to fighting off space aliens.

One reason that the strip was so popular is because it was thought-provoking as well as funny. One of the more well-known strips tells the story of "The Raccoon Incident," highlighting the idea of death through Calvin's eyes as he tries to save a raccoon who is dying.

Watterson's clever writing style and memorable characters make *Calvin and Hobbes* an audience favorite. He focused on themes such as friendship, imagination, and the meaning of life. Although the strip only ran for 10 years, the duo had a lasting impact on popular culture. *Calvin and Hobbes* won 3 Reuben Awards for Outstanding

Cartoonist of the Year, inspired various television specials, and even a video game.

Interesting Fact: Watterson has never allowed the strip to be licensed, because he believed the strip should be enjoyed just as it was. This means that there is no merchandise, toys, or clothing affiliated with the strip. The cartoons can't be used online and only five cartoons per year may be used for educational purposes.

[75]
KRAZY KAT

Along with Garfield and Heathcliff, Krazy Kat was another well-known comic strip kitty. The comic strip appeared in 1913 and continued until 1944. The cartoon was created by George Herriman and appeared first in the *New York Evening Journal*.

In the strip, Krazy Kat is a black, rather simple, happy cat of unknown gender who is completely guileless. Also appearing in the comic strip is a mouse named Ignatz, who is portrayed as short-tempered and mean. Despite the fact that Krazy Kat loves the mouse, Ignatz hates Krazy Kat and spends the entire comic strip planning ways to throw bricks at Krazy Kat's head. Since Krazy Kat is crazed with love, he takes this as a sign of affection.

Another of the strip's characters, Officer Bull Pupp, tries to protect Krazy Kat and throw Ignatz in jail. Eventually, Officer Bull Pupp falls in love with Krazy Kat, just as Krazy Kat falls in love with Ignatz. The zany relationships and antics helped keep *Krazy Kat* popular for a long time.

Interesting Fact: Ignatz the Mouse's famous saying is "Brick me!"

[76]
LYING CAT

Found in the world of the *Saga* comics, Lying Cat plays an important role in working as a lie detector. She appears in the first issue and continues to make an appearance throughout the comics.

Saga is a fantasy comic with a space opera theme that was published in 2012 and continues to be published monthly. While the comic strip did take a break from 2018 to 2022, it's back and as popular as ever. In fact, it's so popular that it has outsold *The Walking Dead* comics. It has also managed to win 12 Eisner Awards, an award for creative achievement in comic books, 17 Harvey Awards, the most prestigious award for comic books, and a Hugo Award for Best Graphic Story.

Lying Cat is a large, blue hairless sphynx that has a unique ability to detect lies. She is "The Will's" faithful sidekick, and when a lie is told she responds by simply saying. "Lying."

Lie detecting is not Lying Cat's only talent — she is also seen taking down oversized men twice her size when the need arises. When she isn't using her claws and teeth to attack her enemies, Lying Cat is much like other cats. Throughout the comic series, it's clear that she wants to be loved and hates to be ignored — like many cats we know. She is known for making funny faces to try and get attention.

Interesting Fact: There is a Funko Pop! Lying Cat Collectible Figure available for interested collectors.

CHAPTER NINE: LITERARY CATS

[77]
BAGHEERA

Bagheera originally appeared in Rudyard Kipling's *The Jungle Book* (1894) and also in *The Second Jungle Book* (1895). He is a black panther who acts as a friend, protector, and mentor to the main character Mowgli, the "man-cub."

Bagheera also appears in the Disney remake of the story that was released in 1967; his character was voiced by Sebastian Cabot. In both the book and the movie, Bagheera is a very important character and the one to originally find Mowgli. Since Bagheera was raised by humans, he is more understanding of the human child than the other animals. He is protective and takes Mowgli to the wolves to be cared for. Despite similarities in the storyline, there are some key differences between the book and the movie.

In the original books, Bagheera was responsible for narrating the story, but in the book, while he still plays the role of Mowgli's protector and guardian, he is not the narrator. Bagheera's dedication to Mowgli has a complete backstory in the book that we don't get to see on screen. This backstory explains why he takes such a liking to Mowgli so quickly. The way Bagheera treats Mowgli is also slightly different. He spoils the child on occasion in the book, but he doesn't do this in the movie. In the original book, Baloo is the strict one and Bagheera gets to cut loose and have fun with Mowgli.

Interesting Fact: The name Bagheera is a Hindi word that means "panther" and an Indian word that means "tigerlike."

[78] BOB THE STREET CAT

Bob became famous after a book was written about him and later turned into a film, spreading his story around the world.

Bob helped a drug addict, James Brown, turn his life around. At first, James tried to return Bob to his owner, but the cat kept showing up, eventually getting hurt. The ginger kitty finally grew on James, who wound up keeping him.

James says that Bob is the reason that he was able to stay off drugs, because he knew his cat needed him more than he needed to give up on life. James sold the story to *The Big Issue*, a newspaper around London, and the two became a popular sight.

James went on to write a couple of books about their friendship and the struggles they faced. The books were named *A Street Cat Named Bob* and *The World According to Bob*. The books were so popular that the movie *A Street Cat Named Bob* was released in 2016 and a sequel, *A Christmas Gift from Bob*, was released in 2020.

Bob passed away in 2020, after he was hit by a speeding car at the age of 15, which led James to start using heroin once again. However, in memory of Bob, James has since become clean again.

Interesting Fact: Bob played himself in *A Street Cat Named Bob*.

[79]
CROOKSHANKS

Another cat from the beloved *Harry Potter* Series is Crookshanks. Belonging to Hermione Granger, Crookshanks is a large orange cat with brown stripes, a bottle-brush tail, and a flat face. With his large size and startling yellow eyes, he is not an attractive cat.

Hermione finds him at The Magical Menagerie and is so affronted that no one wants him because he is ugly, that she decides to adopt him. It's later revealed that Crookshanks is half-Kneazle, which is a magical creature that appears feline and has spotted fur. Along with their looks, they are extremely smart and make wonderful pets for magical people they trust. This makes it hard to get a Kneazle to trust you, since they are very talented at detecting untrustworthy or suspicious people.

In the movie, Crookshanks proved to be quite true to his lineage, helping the young wizards in several situations. For example, Ron Weasley had a long-time pet rat named Scabbers, whom Crookshanks frequently tried to attack. It turned out that the rat was in fact the villain Peter Pettigrew, who had transformed into his animagus form after betraying Harry's parents to Voldemort.

Crookshanks also helps Sirius Black reveal the truth to Harry Potter. He went so far as to steal passwords needed to enter into Hogwarts for Black to gain entrance. Later he led Ron, Hermione, and Harry to the Shrieking Shack where Sirius waited for them. He defended Sirius when Harry attacked him and went so far as to try and steal Harry's wand. When that didn't work, he sat on Sirius's chest to protect him from Harry because he knew that Sirius was a good person and not guilty of all the crimes Peter Pettigrew had pinned on him.

Crookshanks continued to be a huge presence in the books, always showing up around Hermione and her friends. While temporarily separated from Hermione during *Harry Potter and the Deathly Hallows*, they were reunited at the end of the series.

Interesting Fact: It is a well-known theory that Crookshanks once belonged to Lily Potter, because she wanted a cat when Harry was a baby and Crookshanks seemed to already know Sirius Black and hate Peter Pettigrew.

[80]
HODGE

Born in 1709, Samuel Johnson was a writer who was well known for his poems and playwrights but goes on to be titled "arguably the most distinguished man of letters in English history" by *The Oxford Dictionary of National Biography*. However, behind every great man, there is, at least in this case, a cat.

Hodge was one of Samuel Johnson's cats and obviously the favorite, since Johnson took the time to write about him in his book *Life of Johnson*, published in 1971. A majority of the information that we have today comes from that book and the lines Johnson wrote about his cat. Johnson was a self-proclaimed animal lover, but it seemed Hodge had a special place in his heart. Due to his love for Hodge, the cat was mentioned in many other works, including *Life of Samuel Johnson* by James Boswell, *An Elegy of The Death of Dr*

Johnson's Favourite Cat by Percival Stockdale, and *Pale Fire* by Nabokov.

Hodge was mentioned in several of Johnson's writings, including one poem and in Johnson's biography. Percivla Stockdale, a neighbor, wrote about the cat, describing him as having sable fur and always ready to purr when petted.

Interesting Fact: In 1997, there was a bronze statue of Hodge revealed outside of Johnson's home, completed with empty oyster shells beside the cat.

[81]
MACAVITY

Not all cats are on the right side of the law. Originally appearing in T.S. Eliot's poetry book *Old Possum's Book of Practical Cats*, Macavity was a master criminal and con artist.

Macavity was loosely based on the Sherlock Holmes antagonist Professor Moriarty, and just like Moriarty, he was always scheming. In fact, Macavity's poem was the best known out of the book that was Eliot's only attempt to cater to a younger audience. The poem tells us that Macavity, aka the Hidden Paw, is too talented and skilled to ever be caught or leave any evidence behind.

He was described as a ginger cat with a thin body and sunken eyes, and his brow was deeply lined with a domed head and dusty coat. Even his whiskers were uncombed, and he slinked like a snake. His popularity did not stop at the book, and he was brought to the stage in Andrew Lloyd Webber's musical *Cats*, an adaption of Eliot's book. Macavity is the villain in both the book and the musical, referred to as the Napoleon of Crime with untraceable evildoing. Not even Scotland Yard could catch him.

Interesting fact: Eliot also wrote that Macavity has the mysterious ability to levitate, among other possible talents.

[82]
MATILDA

Matilda was a famous cat who starred at the Algonquin Hotel. The Algonquin Hotel was built at 59 West 44th Street in Manhattan, NY. Originally opened in 1902, it features 181 rooms and is well known for some of its famous guests throughout the years, but one permanent guest might be the best known.

The hotel was planned as an apartment hotel focusing on long-term guests, but when Frank Case decided to lease the building in 1907, he changed it into a more traditional hotel. The Algonquin Hotel became famous for its many literary and theatrical guests. Some of the actors who stayed there were Douglas Fairbanks, John Barrymore, Mary Pickford, and Harpo Marx. The writers who stayed there included William Faulkner, Maya Angelou, Gertrude Stein, and J.D. Salinger.

The first owner and manager of the hotel introduced many of the traditions, intending for it to become a literary mecca. Thus, the Algonquin Round Table, a collection of journalists, artists, and writers better known as the Vicious Circle, was founded. Frank Case also decided that a hotel cat was needed to complete the picture, and when a stray cat named Billy came into the lobby unexpectedly, another tradition began. After that, all the female felines who have followed have been called Matilda and all the male cats are called Hamlet. The cats were always rescued from cat colonies or shelters.

In 1986, the first picture of the lineage of cats was taken with Matilda sunning on the front of the hotel. All of the cats of Algonquin Hotel have been treated like royalty, with daily grooming and birthday parties thrown. There has even been a book published about the rags to riches story of Hamlet the cat titled, "Hamlet."

The last Matilda passed away in 2017—she was the third Matilda. The loved ragdoll with long hair and a sweet disposition will be greatly missed. She had retired several years before after 7 years of service and was able to enjoy her loving family in her retirement. The last Matilda was one of the most famous.

Interesting Fact: The most recent cat is an orange tabby named Hamlet.

[83]
MRS. NORRIS

Harry Potter is based around a teen boy who finds out he is a wizard and begins attending Hogwarts School of Witchcraft and Wizardry. At the school, there is a caretaker named Argus Filch who owns a cat named Mrs. Norris.

In the book, Mrs. Norris is a long-haired, scrawny, dust-colored cat with a skeletal body and yellow, bulging eyes. She is portrayed as being extremely loyal to Filch, with whom she has a strong connection. All the kids know that Mrs. Norris will rat them out to Filch as soon as she sees them doing something that he doesn't like. She is a tattle-tail who loves seeing students get into trouble, but despite not being liked by the students, she is beloved by Filch and his closest companion.

In the movies, Mrs. Norris is played by many different Maine Coons, all of them with the typical fluffy coat. Some of the cat actors were Maximus, who plays Mrs. Norris in *Harry Potter and the Sorcerer's Stone*, and Pebbles who is probably the most well-known. Alanis and Cornelius are two other cat actors who also portrayed the noble wizarding cat. All the cats wore matted fur collars and got their hair spiked up with non-toxic hair gel. In many of the scenes, Mrs. Norris has red eyes, which was a digital effect.

Interesting Fact: Mrs. Norris's name came from the Jane Austen novel *Mansfield Park*.

[84]
PUSS IN BOOTS

"Puss in Boots" was originally a fable written by Italian writer Giovanni Francesco Straparola sometime between 1550 and 1553. The story was included in *The Facetious Nights*, a collection of 75 stories and fairy tales.

"Puss in Boots" was about three boys and their mother, who only owns a kneading trough, a pastry board, and a cat. The first time it was published was in 1697 by Charles Perrault in *Histoires ou Contes du Temps Passe*. In his version, the story features a miller who leaves his three boys three things: his mill, his ass, and his cat. Puss in Boots tricks an ogre into turning himself into a mouse that Puss eats. The son who inherited Puss then collects all the ogre's wealth and wins the heart of a princess to boot.

More recently, Puss appeared in the *Shrek* franchise as a cat who wears Corinthian boots, a jaunty black cavalier hat with a yellow feather, a black cape with a silver clasp, and a sword that he is an expert at using. He speaks with a Spanish accent and is voiced by Antonio Banderas. He is an honorable cat with strong morals, and even though he might act on the wrong side of the law, he only does it because he is a survivor at heart.

The first time Puss appears in the *Shrek* franchise, he is a mercenary hired to capture Shrek. However, he ends up befriending Shrek and Donkey. He appears in the *Shrek* movies *Far Far Away Idol*, *Scared Shrekless*, *Shrek the Halls*, *Shrek Forever After*, *Shrek the Third*, and *Donkey's Caroling Christmas-tacular*. He was so popular that he went on to star in four of his own movies.

Interesting Fact: In the original fairy tale, Puss is a fairy that disappears after the happy ending.

[85]
SNOWBELL

Snowbell is the family cat in the book *Stuart Little* by E.B. White, later adapted into multiple movies. The family consists of a father named Frederick, a mother named Eleanor, the oldest child named George, an adopted son named Stuart, an infant named Martha, and a cat named Snowbell. In the movie, Eleanor and Fredrick adopt Stuart, a small mouse, from an orphanage because his parents died by being squished by soup cans. The family works to help Stuart adapt to living as a pint-sized being in a big world.

Snowbell is a Persian long-haired cat and Stuart's best friend, but they don't start out on good footing. Snowbell can't believe that his master is supposed to be a mouse, and initially hates Stuart. He often makes fun of Stuart's small size, which adds some comedic moments to the movie. In fact, he even goes on to try and kill Stuart.

After Stuart joins the Little family, they find a half-frozen songbird named Margalo, whom they save and whom Stuart befriends. Snowbell now has two small animals that he isn't allowed to hunt despite his instincts. In the movie, Snowbell hires someone to eat Margalo, but Margalo finds out about the plot and flees. Stuart borrows a screw-powered motorcycle and goes to find her.

In the first movie, Stuart and Snowbell wind up in many dangerous situations that cause them to start leaning on each other and trusting each other in ways that neither expected. Through their many troubles, Snowbell starts to see Stuart as a family member and not just a nuisance.

Interesting Fact: Nathan Lane is the voice of Snowbell in the first two films.

[86]
THE CAT IN THE HAT

One of the most iconic characters of the beloved Dr. Seuss is the well-known *Cat in the Hat*. The black and white cat with the tall striped hat and a penchant for mischief is a childhood classic.

Dr. Seuss, whose real name was Theodor Seuss Geisel, was born in 1904 and had a happy childhood surrounded by books and art. His father was a zookeeper, and Seuss often visited his dad at work. One of the reasons Seuss grew up to be so whimsical and creative is his father's influence. For example, his father would regularly create complicated and funny inventions like the "Silk-Stocking-Back-Seam-Wrong-Detecting Mirror," which would later show up in Seuss's work as the "whisper-ma-phone," "star-off machine," and many other unusual contraptions.

Seuss went on to attend Dartmouth College and then studied abroad at Oxford University. After returning to the United States, he followed his true passion working as a cartoonist for magazines like *Life* and *Vanity Fair*.

Dr. Seuss started to work on children's books because he loved kids and wanted to create books that helped them learn to read. Unfortunately, he and his wife were unable to have children, which fueled him to pour more of his creative nature into his books. His first book was published in 1937: *And to Think That I Saw It on Mulberry Street*. It was not an easy book to get published and was turned down around 27 times before someone finally wanted to publish it.

The Cat in the Hat appeared in Seuss's second book in 1957 and became an instant success. It takes place in Sally and her brother Conrad's house, where the Cat helps the children escape the rainy-day blues. There are several reasons why *The Cat in the Hat* became so popular, including the memorable rhymes and the life lessons that Seuss's books became so well known for. *The Cat in the Hat* teaches children about their own curiosity and learning how to temper it with responsibility.

Seuss's made-up words and unique worldbuilding are still a childhood staple that encourages creativity in both adults and children. Amongst all his creative works, *The Cat in the Hat* will always occupy a special place in readers' hearts, inspiring movies, cartoons, and even theme park attractions.

Interesting Fact: *The Cat in the Hat* has been translated into over 12 languages, including Latin and Yiddish.

[87]
THE CHESHIRE CAT

When you hear *Alice's Adventures in Wonderland*, you probably think of a little blond girl in a blue frock, but the other characters are just as important. The Cheshire Cat is a character straight out of *Alice's Adventures in Wonderland* by Lewis Carroll, originally published in November 1865.

The name for the character might have been inspired by several different sources: a grinning cat on the west face of St Wilfrid's Church tower in Grappenhall, the British shorthair on the label of Cheshire cheese, and the saying "grin like a Cheshire Cat."

The Cheshire Cat is known for its ability to disappear and reappear whenever he wants, along with his big, wide grin. He is one of the most famous characters in the book, first appearing in Chapter 6 as he helps lead Alice to the Mad Hatter.

He is the Duchess's cat and an important part of the story's plot, but the original book is not the only place where the Cheshire Cat appears. For example, he is also seen on the TV show *Once Upon a Time in Wonderland*. On the show, the Cheshire Cat is a friend of Alice's until Alice leaves. After several years of absence, Alice returns to Wonderland and when she does, the Cheshire Cat is ferocious and loyal to the Red Queen.

The Cheshire Cat became so popular that he is now part of popular culture and can be found in many references. Disney made an adaption of the movie in 1951 with their animated film *Alice in Wonderland*, and again in a live-action 2010 film directed by Tim Burton.

The Cheshire Cat even made it into the video games *American McGee's Alice* and again in *Alice: Madness Returns 2011*. He continues to be a popular character in all genres and formats.

Interesting Fact: The Cheshire Cat can dislocate its head from its body.

[88]
TIGGER

Winnie-the-Pooh written by A.A. Milne is a childhood favorite. The stories and characters became favorites because of the timeless and endearing quality they offer. The writing is beautiful, but simple, making it suitable for children and adults alike. All the stories are wholesome and poignant, delivering messages of friendship and kindness in each one.

Alan Alexander Milne was a veteran of World War I and World War II and worked as a playwright and writer. He wrote *Winnie the Pooh* in 1926 as a way to try and help his child understand the war better. While he wrote many things before *Winnie the Pooh* no one talks about his earlier work.

Winnie the Pooh is still a profitable franchise, making nearly $1 billion in merchandising and surpassing the likes of Mickey Mouse, Donald Duck, and Goofy combined.

Tigger, one of the main characters from the *Winnie the Pooh* books and animated stories, is Christopher's stuffed tiger that comes to life when they go to the 100-acre woods. He's known for his bounding and overly energetic personality. Tigger was introduced as a character in the 1928 story collection *The House at Pooh Corner*. The book was the sequel to *Winnie the Pooh*, published in 1926.

Due to his great personality, Tigger is Pooh's best friend and remains a happy, slightly troublemaking, and not exactly responsible character throughout the series. He is well known for bouncing all over everything and everyone, as well as for his love of fun.

Interesting Fact: Tigger's most iconic scene features him bouncing around the woods singing "The wonderful thing about Tiggers is Tiggers are wonderful things!"

CHAPTER TEN: OTHER NEWSWORTHY CATS

[89]
ALL BALL

While most people have heard of Koko the gorilla, not everyone knows about her best friend who kept her company. Born in 1971 at the San Francisco Zoo, Koko the gorilla spent her life at the Gorilla Foundation, a preserve in the Santa Cruz Mountains. Her full name was Hanabiko as a nod to her birthday, the Fourth of July. In fact, Hanabiko means "fireworks child" in Japanese.

Koko was known for her sign language skills, as she knew a total of over 1,000 different signs and understood an additional 2,000 words in English. Koko started to gain attention when she made a new friend, a kitten that she went on to name All Ball, using her command of sign language. When Koko named the kitten All Ball, it shocked the world because it seemed to prove that Koko could rhyme, an unheard-of ability for an animal.

All Ball was a white and gray Manx kitten, chosen by Koko out of the entire litter. All Ball was carried around like a baby, since Koko never had any children of her own. Unfortunately, All Ball was hit by a car in 1985 when Koko was 13 years old.

Interesting Fact: After All Ball's death, Koko signed "sad bad trouble" and grieved for months.

[90] BART, THE ZOMBIE CAT

Bart became famous in 2015 after being run over and buried before digging his way back out. Ellis Hutson found his cat run over and was so upset that he had a neighbor bury him, thinking he was dead. Five days after the cat had been buried, Bart reappeared, severely injured from the accident.

Hutson took the cat to the Humane Society of Tampa Bay, which had emergency medical funds to help take care of Bart. He had to have an eye removed, his jaw wired back together, and had to now rely on a feeding tube. Originally, Bart was supposed to go home with Hutson after he recovered, but unknown information came to light that led the humane society to refuse to return the cat.

A costly legal battle broke out with Hutson, claiming they were catnapping his cat for publicity. After settling out of court, the humane society got to keep Bart and he was able to stay with the woman who was fostering him with her other three cats. It's obvious she loves Bart very much, and that the two have lived a good life together since Bart arrived in his new home.

Interesting Fact: Bart likes to give head-butts to get scratches, plays with toys he didn't have before, and enjoys eating Boar's Head chicken.

[91]
BLACKIE THE TALKING CAT

In 1981, Blackie the Cat was busy earning a living for his family, Carl and Elaine Miles. The couple was unemployed and without any source of income, so they took to the streets with their talented all-black cat.

Blackie learned how to say phrases like "I love you" and "I want my mama," a skill that attracted crowds to the street who would pay to hear Blackie speak. The public fell in love with him for his unique talent. After a month, the police warned the family that they had to have a business license to continue making money off of their talking cat.

While they did go get a license, the Mileses' considered it unconstitutional for Augusta, Georgia to demand Blackie have a license for public speaking. They claimed it violated his freedom of speech rights. After hearing the case, the judge ruled against them saying no rights had been violated because a cat is not protected by the First Amendment.

The Mileses' went to the United States Court of Appeals. During the trial, it was revealed how Blackie the Talking Cat came to be a talker. Carl told the court how a girl had come by with a box of kittens, which he first declined until a voice told him to take the black one. So, Blackie went home with Carl and when he was five months old, Carl heard a voice again telling him that the cat was trying to talk to him.

Since Carl believed it was the voice of God speaking, he started a speech therapy regimen for Blackie that involved listening to tapes of himself making noise for five hours a day. At six months old, Blackie was talking, but wasn't ready for a public reveal. After a year and a half, he was ready.

The court ruled against Miles and Blackie, claiming that the cat made money and therefore he needed a business license. Since he was not a person, the Bill of Rights did not apply to him. Blackie lived a long life and spent his time talking until he passed away in 1992 at the age of 18.

Interesting Fact: In 1989, Carl got cataracts so Blackie couldn't go out anymore, but his fans started coming to his house to see him.

[92]
CASPER

Born in 1997, Casper was a male cat who became famous for something that most people dread doing: commuting on the bus. Casper was adopted by Susan Fiden when she was 48 years old from an animal rescue center in Weymouth, Dorset in 2002. Casper had been at the rescue for almost a year when Susan came in and fell in love. She originally named him Morse, after a TV show featuring Inspector Morse, but it only took a few days for her to realize there was a better name for her new cat: Casper. He was named after the friendly ghost because he kept disappearing. Thankfully, Susan was happy to respect the fact that he was an independent cat who needed to roam.

On his adventures, Casper didn't appear to be scared of anything. It didn't matter if it was people, traffic, or vehicles. Casper even loved visiting nearby businesses like offices and pharmacies. Realizing that her cat might be too brave and might get hurt, Susan tried to keep him indoors and away from danger. However, nothing Susan did was sufficient to tame Casper's roaming spirit, and he was quickly out and about again.

After the family moved from Weymouth to Plymouth, Devon and Susan went to their jobs as healthcare professionals every day, no longer able to keep up with Casper's escapades. In 2009, Susan found out the shocking truth of what her cat had been doing every day when a bus driver finally clued her in. Each day, Casper would get in line with everyone else and wait for a bus he liked, and, once it arrived, he'd hop in and go sit in his favorite seat. Casper stayed on the bus for the entire 11-mile trip around town and was let off at the bus stop across from his home.

She was so overwhelmed by the driver's and company's kindness to her cat, that Susan wrote a letter and sent it to The Plymouth Herald thanking them. The newspaper was so intrigued, that they wrote an article about Casper, which precipitated his journey to fame as more and more news agencies picked up the story of the amazing commuting cat. The bus company was quick to reassure the world that Casper would never be charged.

Unfortunately, all good things must come to an end. In 2010, at the age of 13, Casper was hit by a taxi driver who didn't stop to help him. Before Susan could get him to the vet, he passed away. Media quickly titled the incident a hit-and-run, and a public outrage followed.

Interesting Fact: Susan Finden wrote a book called *Casper the Commuting Cat* that covers his life and story. It has been translated into six other languages.

[93]
CC (CARBON COPY)

Affectionately nicknamed both CopyCat and Carbon Copy, CC was the first pet to ever be cloned. Texas A&M University used a tabby for her surrogate mother and her genetic mother was a calico named Rainbow.

CC didn't look exactly like her mother due to developmental factors, such as epigenetic reprogramming and x-inactivation, which happens to an embryo before implantation. She was born on December 22, 2001, and five years later she gave birth to four kittens that were fathered by a fellow lab cat. Two of the kittens were boys, one was a girl, and one was stillborn. Their names were Zip, Tim, and Tess.

They were the first offspring of a cloned pet. While most cloned animals seemed to have health problems, CC was remarkably healthy, as were her kittens. She was adopted by a professor at the college, Dr. Duane Kraemer, when she was just six months old. It is thought that being part of a loving household kept her healthy.

CC and her kittens lived in a cat house built in Dr. Kraemer's backyard. She lived to be 18 years old when she passed away from kidney failure, proving to the world that a cloned animal can survive just as long as the original.

Interesting Fact: CC's surrogate mom's name was Allie.

[94]
CHOUPETTE

Even the fashion world is not immune to cats. Choupette, pronounced "shoo-pet," is a well-known figure belonging to the German fashion designer Karl Lagerfeld. After she was born on August 15, 2011, she was given as a Christmas gift to Lagerfeld. Choupette's original owner, Baptiste Giobiconi moved abroad and couldn't bear to give his beloved cat to just anyone.

Choupette is a beautiful blue-cream Birman cat with big blue eyes. During her whirlwind life with Lagerfeld, she got the opportunity to fly on private planes, use her own iPad, and dine out of Goyard dishes. She was featured in international magazines like *Vogue* and appeared in commercials for Opel automobiles and the ever-famous Chanel.

Her blue eyes inspired Lagerfeld to feature her in his Chanel collections, and her creamy coat of fur inspired him to make a matching bridal look. Lagerfeld passed away in 2019, and while he would have liked to have left his fortune to her, French and German law prevented it.

But Choupette was not left without means. She continues to live in Paris with her longtime housekeeper Françoise Caçote. For her 11th birthday, Choupette stood beside a bottle of champagne gazing out the window of a jet. She lives a life more luxurious than most humans.

Interesting Fact: Choupette's name means "sweetie" in French.

[95]
CRÈME PUFF

A famous cat who was a real purring feline was Creme Puff, known as the longest-living cat ever recorded. Born on August 3, 1967, Creme Puff was a domestic cat of unknown breed with a tabby pattern. She was owned by Jake Perry and lived in Austin, Texas. She was a short-haired orange and white cat who lived to be 38 years old and 3 days, passing away in August 2005.

While other cats may have lived longer, none have been recorded. For example, there is a rumor that a cat named Lucy lived to be 39 years old in Britain. There was also another cat owned by Jake Perry who lived to be 34 years and 59 days old. The vet who Jake Perry uses, Bruce Hardesty, says that at least six of his animals have lived to be 30 years old and many more lived to be 25. All of these reports, however, are unofficial, leaving Creme Puff the reigning champion.

With such success, Jake Perry is doing something different. One of the things that he claims is the secret to success is the unique diet that he feeds his felines. Every morning, Creme Puff got broccoli or asparagus, turkey bacon, eggs, and coffee with real cream. It might not be recommended, but it seems to work for his cats.

The other "secret" to the longevity of Jake Perry's cats had to do with the amount of activity they enjoyed. He converted his garage into a movie theater and played nature documentaries that encouraged his cats to stay active and jump around. Then, all along his walls, Jake built stairs and walkways for them to run around on. His cats even had access to an outdoor screened-in area or a "catico," so that all of them could appreciate the outdoors.

Interesting Fact: Every two days Creme Puff got an eyedropper full of red wine and Jake Perry claimed that the wine "circulated the arteries."

[96]
LITTLE NICKY

In 2004, Little Nicky was born, but not in the normal way. Little Nicky was a clone of the original Nick.

In Texas, a lady named Juile loved her 17-year-old Maine Coon so much that she was devastated when he passed away. Instead of mourning her cat, she decided to find a way to get him back and was willing to pay for it. For $50,000, a California-based company named Genetic Saving and Clone was willing to clone Little Nicky. The company ended up shutting down two years later, but they were able to successfully give Julie her Little Nicky back.

While Little Nicky was the first commercially cloned cat, he wasn't the first cat to be cloned. The first cat to be cloned was CopyCat. The thought of paying to have a pet cloned sent several animal support groups like Best Friends Animal Society and Humane Society of United States into moral outrage. They pointed out that the $50,000 would have helped many animals in shelters and on the streets. There was also the fact that Little Nicky had health issues, which the company that cloned him claimed were not genetic, but rather acquired.

Interesting Fact: Little Nicky was physically so close to Nick that he had two identical spots on the roof of his mouth.

[97]
PETER, THE LORD'S CAT

Peter, or the "Marylebone Mog" as he was also known, became famous for his enjoyment of the game of cricket. He lived from 1950 to November of 1964 and could be seen on TV enjoying the games.

Peter seemed to love the attention and publicity that came with being the resident cat at Lord's Cricket Ground in London. While there are no photographs to remember the cricket-loving cat by, there is an obituary. Peter is the only cat to ever be given an obituary in the *Wisden Cricketer's Almanack,* the standard reference book. He was listed as Cat, Peter.

Interesting Fact: Mog is a shortened form of moggy, which is a cat that has no known breed.

[98]
POOH

In Bulgaria, Pooh became the first bionic cat fitted with prosthetics for his back legs. In 2017, after a traffic accident, Pooh lost his back legs. The fluffy black and white cat was forced to use wheels, which would limit his playful nature and put restrictions on his mobility. After a six-month recovery, Pooh was fitted with prostheses, which enabled him to walk and stand as if they were his real legs.

While Pooh was the first cat in Bulgaria to try out prostheses, he wasn't the first cat in the world to do so. In 2009, an all-black cat named Oscar was run over by a harvester near his home in the country of Jersey. He was two and a half years old at the time and was found by a cyclist who brought him to his owners Kate Allan and Mike Nolan.

The couple was referred from the vet to a neuro-orthopedic surgeon Noel Fitzpatrick from the UK. After he looked at the x-rays, Fitzpatrick told them that Oscar would be an ideal candidate because he was only 2 and ½ years old. The couple wasn't convinced at first since the surgery had never been done before, but in the end, he was flown to the UK for his surgery.

The implants were made custom to fit into holes they drilled into his remaining ankle bones. They used a special honeycomb structure so that the skin would grow and bond with it to seal the prostheses. Oscar did have problems three years later when infection kept setting into his right foot, causing the prosthetic to snap off. Once again, surgeon Fitzpatrick came to the rescue, inventing a whole new foot for Oscar and implanting it directly.

Interesting Fact: *Oscar the Bionic Cat* was published in 2013.

[99]
RIJKA

Gaining fame online, Rijka was a beautiful golden longhaired cat with a curious obsession: the vacuum cleaner. Rijka loved her vacuum — while most cats and dogs ran away from the everyday household appliance, Rijka was seen holding the vacuum pole many times.

She became known for holding onto the pole with her front paws and getting her face sucked into it as she licked and played with it. When Rijka got stuck, she would just remove her face from the vacuum like it was an everyday occurrence, which for her it seemed to be.

Her owner, Andrey Lebedev, never expected such an astonishing reaction when he introduced Rijka to the vacuum, but quickly realized how cute it was and filmed it.

Interesting Fact: Rijka comes from Rijks, the Dutch word for rich.

[100]
TOMMASO

Once a stray with no home, Tommaso was found by Maria Assunta, the widow of a property mogul. She immediately fell in love with the solid black kitten.

Assunta was older when she found her new kitten and wanted to make sure that when she passed away, he would be well taken care of. So, when her health began to decline in 2011, she started reviewing many different organizations that could care for the pampered kitty. However, none of them provided the level of care that she was looking for.

In the end, when Assunta passed away at the age of 94, she left everything to her cat with her nurse, Stefania, to care for him. Stefania was also an animal lover, and took such good care of Assunta, that there was no doubt she was the person for the job.

The newly wealthy cat received $13 million and homes in places like Rome and Milan, as well as land in Calabria. Stefania and Tommaso went to live outside of Rome. Her last name and any addresses were never released, so it's unknown how Tommaso is doing with his new family, but he should be well cared for.

Interesting Fact: Tommaso is the Italian version of Thomas.

[101]
WADSWORTH

When Ann Munday found a sickly kitten that was tossed out, she had no idea that he would be with her for many years and go on to help her through some of the biggest challenges in her life.

Ann found Wadsworth (Waddy for short) in Bedfordshire, England after he had been abandoned in critical condition. It took weeks of visits to the vet to combat all the infections that had taken over his body. In fact, he was so small that he didn't have claws on his back feet.

No one at the time knew he would go on to set records by living to be 27 years old, making him the oldest British cat on record. Ann couldn't be happier that she saved him that day because he got her through her husband's passing and many of life's other challenges. She called him "little old man" and made sure she enjoyed his company for as long as he was with her.

Interesting Fact: Wadsworth was named after an English beer.

CONCLUSION

These 101 cats are just the tip of the iceberg. From Garfield and Heathcliff's stunning success in comics, to Stubb's victorious political career, to Félicette influencing the fashion world, cats are running the show whether we realize it or not.

They have influenced and helped shape society in ways that no one could have ever predicted. When cats and humans first started their long relationship, it began an incredible journey that is still benefitting humanity. There is no end to the amazing things that cats can achieve, and many more cats await outside these pages.